Making Lemonade

LEONIE LEWIS

Making Lemonade

A poignant memoir of the struggles and survival of one
woman, and the strength it took to overcome it all

First published in Great Britain, 2020
Amazon Fulfilment

13579108621

A CIP catalogue record for this book is available from the
British Library.

Paperback ISBN 9781710265996

This book is nonfiction. Names, places and incidents may
have been changed to protect the identity of the persons
involved.

Printed and bound by Amazon Fulfilment.

For Marcia – Thank you will never be enough.

For Mum – I never knew the depths of your love until I became a mother. Thank you for being there always. You are Mum. I love you.

For Alissa – Thank you for being my home. Thank you for being my daughter, my best friend and my everything. I have loved you from the moment I started growing you and that love grows stronger every single day.
You are my sunshine. Always and always.

Making Lemonade

Well a big Hi there and Hello to you all. My name is Leonie. I am twenty-seven years old and I have a two-year-old daughter called Alissa. She is my whole world. I love her more than I could ever love anything. I didn't think this amount of love was possible and then I became a Mum. It's a truly incredible feeling. I have had an eating disorder since I was fourteen, along with depression and anxiety. I started this book with the sole intention of talking about my mental health, but as I started writing, I realised I wanted to share so much more with you. My whole journey, my whole fruit bowl of zesty mouldy lemons. Some things I haven't talked about in this book because they're still too raw and painful. Maybe one day though I'll have the courage to face those lemons. Until then, these ones will have to do.

I have a cat named Belle who I love massively. We know each other, we have an understanding. She also taps your hand if you say cheese to her and are holding the cheese. She's practically half dog half wilder beast. I have a lot of tattoos scattered around my body, and they mostly all mean something important to me. I've never smoked, taken drugs or done anything remotely 'cool' or 'out there'. I like to be in bed by eight o'clock in the evenings and I absolutely hate the summer. Rain and knitted cardigans are how I live my best life. I don't think I've ever considered my story interesting but perhaps someone will read it and feel a little less alone. This book covers all periods of my life, from child to teen to my twenties. To being single, married, divorced, pregnant and a Mum. I'm sure at least one person can relate to something. If not, then you're probably reading this book after having bought it in Poundland... That's OK too. Enjoy my dear chums. Enjoy. Leonie.

Life doesn't always work out like you imagined. Life doesn't care what you want and throughout life, you get thrown many lemons. Some of them may be a little hard, some a little too soft, and some full of mould. Life gives you more lemons than you think you'll ever be able to handle and with each lemon it hands out, they can often get heavier, sadder, and more complex.

Life wasn't ready to give me simplicity. It still wanted me to face challenges and wanted to see how I battled and conquered each lemon. That was OK though, because I was strong, and I was fierce. Life wouldn't break me, no matter how many rotten lemons it threw my way.

This is MY story. It's real and raw and it's about all the periods of relapse and all the periods of recovery, and all the mouldy lemons in between. Time to line my lemons up, and blend them one by one, till all I have left is simple, peaceful *lemonade.*

My lemons are not in chronological order, so you'll have to use your minds to navigate back and forth between the years of my life so far. My lemons are not plump and ripe, ready to be cut and sliced for that fresh morning feeling. Most of my lemons are squidgy. Oddly shaped and starting to grow mould. Most of my life so far has really been mould. But my lemons are ripening now and plumping up, filling with fresh life and juice. Things are finally falling into place. Let's go on a journey together so I can finally make my lemonade.

Lemon One

I remember reading Anne Frank's diary as a young girl and feeling so inspired by her story. There was something about the way in which she wrote to Kitty that moved me to the deepest roots of my heart. She wrote with such raw honesty, feeling, and depth that I aspired to be just like her. I felt a strong connection to her, being a Jehovah's Witness till I was fourteen, and knowing that my people also faced the same torment during Hitler's brutal years. I remember being at school in R.E and talking about Anne Frank, and how we wore the purple triangle instead of the yellow star. I remember loving R.E and wanting to teach it.

It's funny how life will always take you back to where you're meant to be. It's so many years later and here I am, at twenty-seven, studying Religious Studies as my degree so I can become the teacher I always wanted to be. Despite all my lemons influencing my career choices, life somehow got me back to my original dreams and ambitions. Anne gave me the courage to not be ashamed of who I was at eleven. I wish she'd stayed with me during my teenage years, but she disappeared and my eating disorder, who I call Ethel, appeared instead and she's been here ever since.

There's so much I need to tell you, so many lemons and although this one came in 2017, I need to tell you about it first. Perhaps because it's so painful and I want to get it out the way or perhaps because he's so precious I want to honour his memory first. I don't know. But this is my first lemon, and it's a real mouldy stinker. This is when my Dad committed suicide.

February 2017 – Dad died

When Dad died, really a part of me died too... Don't panic, I'm not walking around with a bit of flesh missing from my face like a Walking Dead zombie. On the inside though, a tiny spark of my light went out when he left me. As someone who used to suffer greatly from depression, I always thought it would be me who'd take that way out. I was always craving a peace I never found, and always thinking that the world would be better off without me in it.

That day started off as uninteresting as all the rest. I was twenty-four, and five months pregnant. I didn't think I could balloon any bigger than I was. I looked a little like Shamoo the whale and I felt like it too. I can't remember what we, meaning my husband at the time, and myself did. I know it was an ordinary day though, just like any other. It was a Saturday, and we had slipped into a routine of going to the pub down the road for a drink on Saturday evenings, so off I waddled with my starting to swell feet, and we met our friends around seven o'clock that evening. After a few hours of happiness and laughter, I got a phone call from my Nan. It was so loud in the pub I didn't answer. I went downstairs to the toilets and rang her back, thinking something must have happened because she would never phone me at nearing ten o'clock. I never thought I'd hear what I heard though.

"Your Dad's killed himself."

Not sure what to do when you're in a pub that's heaving with drunk people and your Nan tells you your Dad is dead... Like a typical polite Brit, my response was something along the lines of,

"OK."

When I had ended the call, I burst into tears. I text my husband to come down and find me and then he had to huddle me out of the pub like an A list celebrity because I couldn't control my crying, or my breathing. My then husband text our group of friends to all leave so I didn't have to face them, and I just remember waddling home, clutching to my growing bump, because in that moment, I didn't want to lose her too.

Dear Dad

I thought I'd write you a series of letters to talk about life after you left us, and perhaps maybe memories of life when you were still with us, I don't know yet. The good thing about writing, is that you never quite know where you're going to end up. I intended on writing about you first and made you my very first chapter. I think I did that because you're my biggest heartache in amongst all this mould I've accumulated over the years. Funnily enough though, you've ended up being the last chapter I'm writing, because I couldn't bring myself to open this lemon. I don't even want to think about what you must have been going through that Saturday morning, afternoon and evening – I'm not sure when exactly you took your life, and I don't want to imagine you hanging there all day long before you were found, but I believe this is what happened. I wonder if you woke up that day and thought about your unborn grandchild. You only had to wait a matter of days to find out if I was having a boy or a girl, but you couldn't hang on long enough. That hurts me down to my very core, because this grandchild of yours, she's the most precious thing in the world Dad, and you would have absolutely *cherished* every ounce of her being.

Like I said, I've not been able to write about you until now, on September 9th, 2019. It's a Monday and nothing special has clicked in my brain to make me start typing, but I suddenly thought, instead of trying to write what happened, which feels too painful and raw, why don't I just focus on writing to *you*. So that's what I'm going to do Dad, I'm going to spend this chapter, writing *to* you, and not *about* you. I'm going to write you all sorts of things Dad, because since you've been gone, so much has happened, and you need to know it <u>all</u>.

My love, always,

Leonie

Dear Dad

The first letter I wrote you was handwritten, and I wrote it before Alissa was born and it read this.

"I'm sorry I wasn't there enough, I'm sorry I didn't make the effort to try and come and see you. I didn't help and support you and I guess it was because I was still so angry with you for hurting me so much. I'm not angry at you now, I just miss you. I'd give *anything* to have you back. I'd do all the things I should have done whilst you were alive and suffering. I'd come and see you and support you and phone you every day and send you cards and do whatever it took so you knew I was always there, and you weren't alone. I can't do any of that stuff now, but I can write to you and tell you I love you. I can tell you I'm having a little **girl** and maybe she'll suck her thumb just like me and sleep all day and I'll call her Noddy too, so a bit of you stays with me always. We're calling her Alissa-Rose. There will only ever be one person missing from her life and that'll be <u>you</u>, her Grandad. I'm sorry we only had one walk around Redhill Park together and I'm sorry if it felt as though I never had or made time for you. I took for granted that you'd always be here and now you're gone, and I miss you and there's just a hole in my heart where you should still be. You weren't the best Dad, but you were <u>my</u> Dad. I'll love you, and I'll carry you with me, always. Love your Noddy."

Dear Dad

I'm going to just get this letter out the way quickly and write about the evening I found out you'd died. Nan phoned me and told me and I don't remember what I said then or how the phone call ended, but I remember her telling me I needed to get hold of Ashleigh (because she was abroad travelling) and I remember phoning Mum and then telling Frankie and crying. There was a lot of crying. Frankie bundled me out of the pub and somehow, I walked back home. We were living in the two-bedroom flat in Winton at the time, the one you liked, and the pub was just a few minutes away down the high street. When we got through the front door, I sat on the edge of the bed and I cried for what felt like forever. I had makeup on, and I thought about all the things I needed to do, to get me and bump ready for bed, and all the people I needed to tell. Plans I needed to cancel, trying to get hold of Ashleigh, and the daunting anxiety of all the things that would follow on from this. After I managed to stop crying, I told Frankie we'd need to cancel seeing our friends for lunch the next day, and can you believe he said "really?" … REALLY?! No, let's go out for a merry old lunch shall we. I was angry at him for being so insensitive and almost acting as though it was no big deal that you were gone.

I got into my pyjamas, took my makeup off, went to the loo, cleaned my teeth, and then sat on the sofa in the lounge and sent text messages to all the people I loved. I told Lauren and Megan, my two best friends, and my dear friend Marcia to cancel the plans we had to meet up. The responses made me cry all over again and my eyes became puffy and heavy. I went to bed crying, and I woke up crying, thinking it was a bad dream. The realisation that it was real, based on how awful I felt and how puffed up my eyes were, made me cry even more.

The next day, Frankie told me although we weren't going for lunch, we still had to drive an hour away to his friends so he could fill up his water tank for work Monday. He was still doing your window cleaning round at the time Dad, looking after all your old customers, which I recently found out were Grandad's old customers, which is nice. We started the drive and I remember thinking this was *not* what I needed right now, but at the same time, I needed to be with Frankie, because I had his child growing inside me, and I needed him to be my rock. We drove and drove, and I started to spread the news a bit wider, telling a few other friends and trying desperately to get hold of Ashleigh. Somewhere along the way, Ashleigh rang, and we had to pull over so the Internet signal would stay so I could tell her. I didn't want to be the one to tell her, but I also *had* to be the one to tell her. It was my responsibility because there were only the two of us that belonged to you, and it was my job to tell her our Dad was dead.

I felt powerless telling my big sister that you were gone Dad, and not being able to hug her or say anything of any comfort. She was so far away, and she needed Mum, but she had to grieve for you alone. You left us at the worst possible time, when one child was all alone in a different country and your other child was heavily pregnant and needed you more than ever. But there we go Dad, we can't change what's happened, can we?

After the second day, things started to settle in a bit more that you were gone. Ashleigh kept trying to find flights home, and eventually got one booked. I started getting phone calls from Nan to start organising things and all your mail suddenly started coming to me to sort out, because Ashleigh wasn't here, and I was your daughter.

I started to feel overwhelmed Dad, there was so much to do, and I had never done anything like this before. With an administration-based background or not, nothing prepared me for having to sit there opening your post and responding to your letters. I had to go through all your bills, debt collector letters, bank statements, volunteer information and email them one by one to tell them you were gone. I had to also keep studying for my Level 3 course in Counselling and work from home. I could barely carry myself anymore, not just the physical strain of being pregnant, but the mental and emotional heaviness I felt having to be the one to sort everything out and stay on top of everything.

When Ashleigh came home, it was like the responsibility had already been given to me, so I just kept it all. I carried on emailing debt collectors and informing the places you'd enquired or started volunteering at, and I then had to go into your bank and sort out your finances and then arrange your funeral. Everything was hard and heavy, and I felt all alone, despite being surrounded by people. Frankie got to a point of being almost fed up that I was *still* grieving. Can you believe Dad, he was *annoyed* that he had to come to your funeral? He didn't want to take the day off work. I couldn't believe the person who was meant to love me wholeheartedly and who I'd married and loved despite everything, couldn't even hold me and carry me through this trauma.

Your funeral took place at the Kingdom Hall, which is exactly where it should have been. Nan arranged that for us, and me and Ashleigh used the money you left behind to arrange your cremation and the collection of your ashes, which me and Frankie collected. When the funeral came around, I don't think I was prepared for it and I just felt embarrassed to be there, because I felt so huge. Alissa by that point was stretching my stomach out so much, and I remember Mum saying I looked big in my funeral dress. This just filled me with worry, and I didn't want everyone looking at me, but I knew they would be. When we arrived at the Kingdom Hall, I couldn't believe how many Jehovah's Witnesses had turned up for you. The hall was full of your brothers and sisters who all wanted to remember you and be there for us. As soon as I walked in, everybody started coming up to me, either with condolences, or with "do you remember me… no you wouldn't, you were only small…" or with "oh, how far along are you, may I…" followed by lots of touching of the bump. I was surrounded by people and although they were loving people, I just wanted to escape. We had to sit at the very front and I felt everyone's eyes on me, and I didn't want to be there at all. I didn't feel like it was a goodbye to you, perhaps because we didn't say goodbye or maybe because it wasn't a typical dark and depressing funeral, I don't know. Either way, I think you'd have been happy with your funeral Dad. It was about love and peace and everyone who was there, was there to comfort us and remember you. I think that's the way you'd have wanted it. It was like Grandad's funeral but this time I wasn't grieving for Grandad and you weren't grieving for your Dad, I was grieving for my own Dad.

Even months after you were gone, letters kept coming for you, and they were a constant reminder that you weren't here anymore. I kept forgetting that you were dead and thinking you were just in your little room, half an hour away. The biggest physical challenge we had was sorting out your room and clearing it out so your landlord could re-let it. I'm very grateful to Frankie for his help that day and to Ashleigh, because I couldn't do any lifting at all, and I could barely walk up and down the stairs. I made sure that me and Frankie arrived first, because I wanted to have a look around and find the big fleece jacket of yours that you always wore, and I always wanted. I found it and I still have it, along with your hat, but they no longer have your smell on them, and I miss it. When we walked into your room, the police had left the noose you'd made and suddenly it was very real, and I could visualise you hanging there. They said you wouldn't have felt any pain because of the amount of morphine you'd taken, but I don't know if I believe them. I don't know if you can have a completely pain free death. I hope and pray you did.

The days and weeks, and even the months, following your death were physically demanding. They were emotionally and mentally traumatic and they are days I will never forget.

I'm so thankful that those immediate days are over, because trying to reflect on them and remember them to write about, is painful. It's been well over two years now since you took your life, but the pain of your absence is real and raw.

My love, always,

Leonie

Dear Dad

The only bit of happiness just after you'd killed yourself, was going to the hospital with Mum, Daisy and Frankie, and finding out I was having a beautiful baby *girl*. I want to tell you about that memory Dad, because if you'd been alive, I'd have phoned you to tell you, and I think you'd have been happy for me. We found out she was a girl on February 21st, 2017, just three days after you left. Alissa was born on the 21st July 2017 and so the number 21 now means something special to me, with the 18th being something sad for me, with both you and Grandad dying on the 18th. That Tuesday we arrived at the hospital and Mum and Daisy came with us. Mum had bought baby clothes and she was so adamant it was going to be a girl, she said she'd only bought girls clothes. I knew in my heart Alissa was always a girl because I couldn't ever imagine myself having a boy. I think I'd have been disappointed if my scan revealed a boy, and I was so relieved when the sonographer said, "I'm pretty sure she's a girl." She couldn't be one hundred per cent sure because little Alissa bean was wriggling around in my tummy so much with her legs firmly crossed and she only got a quick glimpse. My Mum was thrilled and when we left the room, she then told us she'd bought a neutral outfit 'just in case.' We were all happy and I was so excited, I just had to post it on Facebook but with that, I also had to write about you Dad. I had to tell all our friends you were gone, and that only made it more real that whilst I was so happy, I was also breaking inside. You left me when I needed you but it's not your fault because I don't think you ever knew how much I needed you. How much I loved you, cherished you and adored you. Our relationship over the years had been full of disappointment and hurt, resentment and sadness. Then we found a peace with one another and we rebuilt our relationship, and I'm so thankful we were able to do that before you left. I think you knew how much I loved you, but I can never be sure and that's probably one of the most painful things I must deal with now. I will never know if you knew just how loved you were by me and Ashleigh. We only ever told you the bad things and blamed you for our childhood sadness, but we never told you the good things about you, or the happy memories we had of you growing up. Maybe you never knew what you meant to us, both as children and as adults. I'm so sorry if you didn't know. I'm sorry if you never knew that you were *our* Dad and we loved you unconditionally.

My love, always,

Leonie

Dear Dad

In my quest to find lemonade, I've had to do an awful lot of self-reflection and a lot of healing. It's been hard to heal from you, and I'm still not there yet. I think this is because you're not here so I can't talk to you and go through all the trauma that I've experienced. One day in school, my teacher asked me what I would like as an ideal situation and I remember telling her I would love to have you and Mum back together so we could be a 'proper' family. I don't think I really meant it, but the point I want to make from it, is that you were *always* in my thoughts. Even as a teenager going through real mental illness, I wanted nothing more than to have you as my Dad, a constant father figure, there to hug me and hold me whilst I cried. The fact that you only saw us once a week, if that, was painful and remained painful for a long time. I felt as though you didn't love us enough and you didn't care if you saw us or not. Being an almost thirty-year-old adult, I can now see that you did in fact love us in your own way, all along. You may not have been a constant rock of support, and you may not have been there every day, but you didn't ever give up. You didn't ever become a permanent absence and although you put your life ahead of ours, you tried your best. Healing from the hurt you caused as a child has only recently happened, and what's made me heal has been reading all your cards. Another of my biggest regrets is throwing away the card you wrote me when I had chicken pox when I was little. I'll never forget the card, because for years it remained in my memory box, and I would hug it on the days when I missed you terribly and on the days when you'd cancel seeing me and Ashleigh. You'll remember it, an A5 landscape card, with a brown background and a dog on the front. You got Ashleigh a similar one. I don't remember throwing it away and I didn't think I would have done because like I said, it was extremely precious to me. I can only think that when we fell out in 2016 over Frankie taking on your window cleaning business, I must have thrown it away out of anger and sadness. I wish I'd kept it. All your cards end with "all my love, Dad." Often, you'd write something like "never forget your Dad loves you" and a lot of the time you'd start them with "Noddy." Reading through the cards I have that you wrote me, from a get well card to my engagement and anniversary cards, has made me see and realise that you've always loved us and you were sorry for the mistakes you made.

Being a mother now, I can see that as a parent, you can only do your very best, and you can only do what you think is right, at the time. You make mistakes, and perhaps those mistakes will stay with your child forever, but whatever mistakes you make, the love you have for your child is rock solid and will never fade. The love I know you had for us, has helped me to heal from the pain that you caused me as a child and at some points in my adult life. I know you loved me with all your heart, and I'm sorry it's taken your death for me to realise it.

My love, always,

Leonie

Dear Dad

My head is bouncing through all our memories, and I can't think of one that I want to write about. We've made lots of memories throughout the twenty-four years of my life you were alive for, but I don't know what I want to tell you about them. I wonder how much my memory differs from your memory of the same day. I wonder how you felt about a day and how I felt about that same day. I often sit and think of you and wonder what you'd think of my life now, of what it's become. I've written about Frankie next in this book, but I think I want to tell you what happened. I think you deserve to know. At the time of your death, Frankie and I were 'happily' married. You didn't know what had happened in 2015, in the following months after our wedding and as far as you were concerned, we were happy and in love. So, Dad, I should probably tell you something that I should have told you when you were alive. Frankie had been messaging other women since the very start of our relationship in 2013, right up until our wedding day on August 21st, 2015. I found out about it in October 2015, and he broke my heart. I didn't tell you then because I wasn't sure what your reaction would be. I didn't think you'd be one of those Dad's who'd go all 'Rambo' as you used to put it and go beat him up. I suppose I didn't think you'd have a reaction at all. I thought perhaps more than anything, you may understand *him*, being a man and perhaps understanding his desires. I think I thought back then that maybe you'd just tell me it was normal, and I should just stay with him and work things through. I did this anyway and stayed with him until February 2018, a year after you died. My heart was broken and when you blew up at Frankie over the window cleaning, I took Frankie's side because I'd already decided to stick with him, and I was still in love with him. I regret not supporting you and your disappointment in him at the time, and I wish the situation hadn't caused you and I to fall out so massively. You put a note through my door telling me how angry you were at him, and how if you killed yourself it would be on my shoulders. I didn't speak to you for a long time after that and you hurt me, almost to the same level that Frankie had hurt me.

Thinking about it now, it of course doesn't matter in the slightest. I'd give anything to have you here to put that same letter through my door. I'd rip it up, come knock on your door and hug you and tell you not to be so stupid. That Frankie was the idiot, not me and not you and that don't you dare ever even *think* of killing yourself because I love you and I need you. Of course, none of that happened and none of that will happen now. We finally made up after a long chat at Nan's house and you came to my door and told me you were sorry. You brought cake round and we hugged and cried, and things were OK again. I wish I'd known then that I'd only have you in my life for one more year, and then you'd be gone.

My love, always,

Leonie

Dear Dad

I'll never be ready to say goodbye to you, but now the good thing is, I don't have to. Your death made me think about what I want for myself and for Alissa and for our future. It wasn't long after your death that I found one of your old suicide letters on your memory stick. You didn't leave us a note when the time came, so I think all the letters in the years before were cries for help. We never thought you'd kill yourself. We should have taken every single cry for help seriously and gotten you as much help as we could. We didn't. We, *I*, let you down. I'm sorry. That letter I found had a request from you on it, I don't know if you'll remember, but you asked me and Ashleigh to each have a Bible Study. You'd gone back to the meetings then and I truly believe you were firm in your faith again, as a Jehovah's Witness. You asked something very small of me and Ashleigh, and so it seemed only right to do it for you. It wasn't just that which made me decide to start going to the meetings again. Mum had been going for a while and Mum's friend Jan had said to me during a conversation, that if there was even a slight chance of everything the Bible said being true, why wouldn't I want that for Alissa. It got me thinking about what I believed in and what I wanted for my daughter. Nothing would bring me greater happiness than you getting to meet her, in the new system. So, for the last, I'm not sure how many months now, I have been going to meetings again, and I have been having a weekly Bible Study. My faith is strong, and with it I have found a peace and a love I never thought possible. I've realised that you were right all along when you said if there's nothing to look forward to at the end, why are we even bothering now. You were so sad, and I never saw it. My eyes weren't open then, but they are now. I'm back in the faith I grew up in, the one I left for thirteen years, and the one I now call home. You were a big part of my return to Jehovah, and I can only ever say thank you for that Dad. I can't wait till the day we get to all meet again, the day when Alissa can finally look up, see you and call out "Grandad."

My love, always,

Leonie

Dear Dad

I think this is probably going to be my last letter to you. I wasn't sure where I'd end up writing to you, whether I'd want to write about all my childhood memories or write letters of blame and resentment or write letters of grief and apology. It turns out I just wanted to write to you. It didn't really matter what, what mattered was letting myself feel all the pain of your passing, and all the love that I know you had for us. Two and a half years later and I still miss you every single day. I still grieve for you and I still long for your presence. You're gone and this lemon you've left me with, is stinky and rotten. You've left a mould that I don't think will ever go away, but it's starting to change colour. I'm starting to understand grief more and understand that feeling the pain and the sadness is OK. It's all part of healing. I don't need to let you go, and although life carries on, I don't need my life to *move on*, away from you. I want to carry you with me, everywhere I go. I've always loved this poem, by E.E. Cummings, and now, more than ever, it has a special place in my heart, because I will *always* carry you with me.

> *"i carry your heart with me (i carry it in*
> *my heart) i am never without it (anywhere*
> *i go you go, my dear; and whatever is done*
> *by only me is your doing, my darling)*
> *i fear no fate (for you are my fate, my sweet) i want*
> *no world (for beautiful you are my world, my true)*
> *and it's you are whatever a moon has always meant*
> *and whatever a sun will always sing is you*
>
> *here is the deepest secret nobody knows*
> *(here is the root of the root and the bud of the bud*
> *and the sky of the sky of a tree called life; which grows*
> *higher than soul can hope or mind can hide)*
> *and this is the wonder that's keeping the stars apart*
>
> *i carry your heart (i carry it in my heart)"*

You may have left behind a sadness that will never fade, and you may have left at a time when we really needed you to stay. You may have left selfishly, but it was because you just couldn't hold on anymore. You were done with life and you needed to escape. I understand that feeling more than you'll ever know and I am so grateful that I don't feel that darkness anymore. The fact is though, that you *did* feel that way and those feelings were real to you. We let you down and we didn't give you enough love, encouragement and support.

Life after you has been really hard and full of ups and downs. I think you'd be proud though, Dad. Proud of the journey I've been on, from when you were alive, to now, and proud of where I am in my life. I'm happy. I'm almost free of all these lemons, and I've worked hard to make a good life for me and for Alissa. Mum's been a huge support and I wouldn't have survived without my closest friends. I may have lost you, and Frankie, and Grandad too years ago, but I've gained so much too. I've gained the most beautiful girl in the whole world and she's two now Dad, and she's remarkable. She loves stories and reads all the time. She loves dancing around the kitchen, and she loves it if you pick her up and fly her around the flat like Buzz from Toy Story. She loves chocolate and she will still climb into my bed halfway through the night for cuddles. She loves Belle the cat and I'm glad she likes dogs too because I had such a fear of them until a few years ago and I didn't ever want her to be afraid of them. Alissa is such a kind child, and she always says please and thank you and every night she says her own little prayer which is adorable to listen to. She loves Mum and Frankie's Mum so much and there's three photos of you in my/your Bible and she always says Grandad when she sees them. She *knows* you and she will know all mine and Ashleigh's funny stories of you when she's older. We'll teach her the garden worm song and we'll tell her all about driving in your hideous vans along Ashley Road, and how you hated traffic. We'll make our memories, *her* memories, and you'll be as real to her as though you were just down the road.

There's so much you've missed out on since your death, and that's only two years. It makes me sad to think of all the memories I'll create with Alissa that won't have you in. It makes me sad to think of all the joy you could have brought Alissa, with your funny faces and ridiculous humour. Your death has just made me so *sad*. It's OK though, because although the sadness is great, the love and the memories are greater. You may just be a statistic to the world, but to your family, and to me, you'll forever be, **Dad**.

My love, always,

Leonie

Lemon Two

Although not my most painful lemon, this is certainly one of my biggest ones. This lemon is all about meeting who I thought was the absolute love of my life, and who turned out to be the biggest let down out of everybody. In 2012 I started working at a school for children with special needs. I was a teaching assistant and for the first time ever, I felt like I had a 'proper career' and my life was sorted. I got to spend every day working with one of my best friends and although hard work, it was the most rewarding job I've ever had. One day, not long after I started, I noticed the smile of a cheeky looking young man. He was shorter than my five feet and eleven inches frame, and not what I thought I would be attracted to, but somehow, he managed to draw me in. He had a look about him that was intriguing, and I found myself wanting him to see me and notice me. One day whilst walking down the corridor with my best friend, he passed us and said a brief hello and my bestie – who I'd met at college, four years earlier, told me he was a player and to stay away. Of course, she was right, but at the time, I couldn't let go of him. It was a strange feeling really because I hadn't had any lengthy conversations with him at that point, he hadn't shown an interest in me and yet, I found myself looking for him every day I went to work.

I had to do a basic sign language course and it was held after school once a week for a few months. It just happened to fall on a Wednesday and our class had swimming the hour or so before the school day ended. Each week I would turn up with wet frizzy hair and no makeup on, and I remember walking in the first day and who should be there but this cheeky man again, Frankie. I could tell straight away the other girls liked him, a little too much, and he certainly enjoyed the attention. I couldn't help myself though, I was so drawn to him and taken in by his smile and his personality. For some unknown reason, out of all the stunning women who worked at the school, he decided to take an interest in *me.*

Our story begins there and ends somewhere messy, six years later. There's so much to talk about and I don't even know where to begin. I can't remember our first 'date' but I can tell you about some of our first 'moments.' It must have been a few weeks into the sign language course, and Frankie had started saving a seat for me next to him and looking for me at lunchtimes and at playtime in the playground. The school had two separate buildings opposite each other, and he'd started waving to me from across the road, in the building he worked at. He'd come over to my side at lunch and look for me in the staffroom. I still didn't think much of it, I knew he couldn't *like* me because I was fat and tall, with frizzy hair. I didn't know how to flirt, and I wasn't cool and didn't go out drinking or dancing or wearing little skirts and high heels. I just went to work, went home, watched TV and went to bed. Something about me made him choose me though.

Now I look back, I look at it like he was choosing prey, a victim, an easy target. Why go for the confident, sexy blonde when you can go for the insecure, fat girl? He would often wait for me outside school in his long red Astra and I'd always come up with an excuse as to why he couldn't come back to mine. I was anxious about being together outside of work, but he didn't fall for my lies, and waited for me to walk past, then rolled down his window and looked at me with his sparkly eyes. He came to my flat and told me all about his exciting life as a co-driver for rallies. He told me about all the adventures he went on and the pubs he'd go to regularly and the nights out he'd have. It all sounded so new and exciting and I remember feeling so small in comparison (not physically obviously!)

I can't think how we became a couple really, I can just remember a few key memories like him telling me in the staffroom about his cheating ex-girlfriend and how he had trouble trusting and loving people. I remember him giving me chocolate through the playground gate to cheer me up. I remember on Valentine's Day he'd found a card somewhere and wrote a cheesy message inside and put it in my locker. I remember we went to a little bar close to my flat, where I felt safe with my anxiety, and I told him I had an eating disorder and I was pretty messed up and he shouldn't get involved with me, but he didn't mind. He saw past all of that and seemed to like me, for who I was. It made me feel like maybe I was something special after all, maybe to this fantastic man, I could be something *more*. After our drink, we went for a walk to the over cliff, to watch the waves crash as they washed in and out on the beach and we watched the sunset. I felt beautiful and we both told each other we had a secret. It turned out it was the same secret – we were both quitting work and our last day was on the same day.

It all felt like 'fate', like we were meant to be together. When we left work, I think we officially became a couple. We were inseparable, and for the first time, he took me to meet his Mum. I knew she was special to him from the way he spoke about her, I knew he valued her opinion a lot, and I knew I wanted her to like me. Frankie made a bet with me that his

Mum would hug me as soon as she met me and I didn't need to be worried whether she'd like me, he knew she would. When we got there, I was so nervous because I was already so in love with this beautiful man, and I wanted her to love me too and feel I was worthy of her son's affections. We walked in and she had her husband round, and so she didn't hug me, and Frankie lost the bet. We laughed about it for ages afterwards because I came to learn that she absolutely would have hugged me on that first meeting had she not been busy, because she is the definition of love and care and all things snuggly.

After that we seemed to spend every free day we had together. Frankie started a job at a pub and so started working nights. I'd stay up till he had finished work at two in the morning and then the next day we'd have the whole day together to go on adventures. He didn't care about driving far away or for long periods of time. We'd go to Devon just to put some stickers on a rally car he'd be sitting in for an event coming up. We'd drive an hour just to get to a pub and then another hour just to go watch the sunset somewhere near trees and hills and the beautiful world. Everything became so beautiful with him in our first year, and I was so in love with him, probably from the first month we were together.

He was the first, and only man I've ever slept with and the first time we slept together, I wanted everything to be perfect. He had spent the day with me, and I was wearing a dress I knew he'd love, because at some point during our time at work, he'd mentioned that he loved hearts on clothes. I bought a black floaty dress that had little white hearts all over it. I remember him looking at me all day and feeling butterflies in my stomach because I knew, without a doubt, that it was time and I was ready, and he was the one. He had to work at the pub from six or seven, but he promised he'd come back after his shift. When he got in around two in the morning, I was wearing an oversized shirt with my makeup on of course and pretended to be asleep. He got into bed and 'woke me up' with soft kisses and after we had sex, I knew I didn't ever want to be without him.

Not long after that night, he drove me to what had become 'our' pub and he wrote 'I love you' on something like a beer mat, or a piece of paper or a bit of a map he had, I can't quite remember. We both loved going on these adventures and we both seemed to want the same things. I'd found my *one*. I knew then that I would marry this man, and I waited a very long three years for that day to come.

I know the beginning of a relationship is always special because it's new and exciting. You're figuring out what you both love together, and what you both love about each other and each other's individual hobbies, and you spend every moment together laughing and having *fun*. The hard stuff comes later but I still think to this day, that what we had at the beginning of our relationship was deeper and more precious than anyone's beginning stages. It was like we were made for one another, and we could do whatever we wanted in life, if we were together. Everything about us led me to believe that we were fated to be together, like Romeo and Juliet. We both had a health and social care background, and that led us to working at the same school. We both grew up as Jehovah's Witnesses and we both stopped going to the religious meetings when we were teenagers, although he is seven years older than me. Our families were all sort of connected from the religion and my Mum even found a photo of me with his sister when we were younger.

Probably a year in, I started to notice little things about him that made me feel insecure and anxious. I'd visit the pub he worked at and notice the way he chatted to a couple of his colleagues. The way he'd flirt with them, and with the customers, in the same cheeky way he'd captured my attention. I started to realise he wasn't over his previous girlfriend. We were out driving one evening and he saw her car being driven by her new boyfriend and started chasing the car down the road, hoping to see her. He'd ask me to wear 'nice' outfits for occasions when we *might* run into her. I started realising that although he gave me wholesome true love, with that came an overwhelming sense of worry.

I pushed the thoughts and feelings that he wasn't as committed to me as I was to him deep down, until they disappeared and the love I felt for him could continue to thrive. He had done so much for me, taken me out of my comfort zones, taken me on adventures across the country, helped my eating to get better, and helped me to feel sexy at the size I was at the time. He helped me to feel more confident in so many different ways and helped me to feel so much love. We started dating properly in February 2013, and by my birthday in May, I was ready for him to propose to me. I loved him more than I could have ever imagined loving another human… boy was I wrong (but I'll get to Alissa later).

Dating Frankie meant going out in the evenings, going to pubs, seeing his friends, socialising, going to rallies, staying out all day, going out to eat, staying away spontaneously overnight, and experiencing new things every day. It was exciting and scary, but when I was with him, I didn't feel so anxious. He managed to make me feel invincible and I loved him more with every passing second.

In December 2014, on Christmas Day, I woke up to a present hunt around the flat we were living in. That hunt led to various presents and then to my main present, which was a bottle of CHANEL perfume. Over the time we'd been together, I'd been let down by him on special occasions because he never had any money to spend on me. He never saved or thought about buying gifts, and so when I got to my bottle of perfume, I felt so happy that he'd spent *actual* money on me, and thought of something I'd really like, (instead of earmuffs that doubled as earphones which was my birthday gift… a slight disappointment when you are hoping for a ring.) I didn't realise there was one final clue on my perfume bottle, that led me to a ring inside a Christmas cracker. That day he finally proposed and I felt the happiest I'd ever felt.

There had been two big moments before this Christmas where I thought he was going to pop the question. One time we were at the rally of his dreams, and I'd paid a considerable amount of money for him to do it, because he didn't have any. I'd used my savings for him instead of for the driving lessons I had planned to take, and there was a big opening ceremony. His sister had said he was going to propose so I made sure I looked my absolute *best* and got ready to be given the best gift of all. When the evening ended and nothing had happened, I felt a great sadness, but more than that, a great disappointment. The next time was on a stay away my Mum had got us as a gift, where we stayed in a fancy hotel for two nights and I thought for sure he was going to do it then. When the mini break came to an end with no proposal, I felt the same huge wave of disappointment and I realised that lately he'd been filling my life with more negativity.

We started having big arguments and they were becoming more frequent. I knew he was cheating on me, but time and time again he'd deny it. He would keep his phone glued to him twenty-four seven and suddenly, a password lock appeared on the front screen that hadn't been there before. I knew it in my gut, but the love I felt for him was so deep, that I couldn't let myself leave. There are a few memories I have of my suspicions, but the gut feeling was there all the time after a little while. The first one I remember was his phone going off early in the morning and the noise woke us up. He read it but hid it from my view and then put his phone face down. When he fell back to sleep, I got up and took his phone downstairs to find it was a message from his previous girlfriend. I was filled with anger and bitterness. We argued and he denied anything happening, any communication between them, and convinced me it was just a one off out of the blue message.

The next key memory I have is in a different flat but same story. A girl he was 'just friends with' sent him a photo message with a caption reading "bath time." I saw the caption but not the photo and started an argument once again. It turned out she'd sent a photo of a rubber duck in the bath, but the following photo after that one was a photo of her. I knew then that he'd been lying to me for months, but I didn't want to leave him.

These incidents spanned over months, so you can imagine the build-up of stress, anxiety and insecurity. All the feelings you feel when you know the person you love more than anything is cheating on you, but you're not brave enough or strong enough or independent enough to leave. My best friend had to rescue me many times at midnight for a quick McDonald's milkshake with a side order of insane crying.

It was in the same flat as the ducky photo that Frankie proposed to me and soon after that we moved flats and I relapsed heavily in my eating disorder. I will talk about this in a moment but while deception and lies are on my mind let's just get the big one out the way and then we'll work backwards in time to the relapse, before I found out. In our new flat, we had eight months until our wedding in August and then we were married. In October, two months after our big day, Frankie had a weeklong rally in Italy. I didn't want him to go because I was suspicious and knew I couldn't trust him, but also because I loved him, and we were newlyweds and I wanted him with me. I decided for Christmas I'd buy him a new phone because his had broken and he was so upset about losing all his photos. I ordered the same phone off eBay and it came in that week he was away. I decided to put the memory card from his broken phone into the new phone and set it all up ready so when he opened his present it was ready to go and he'd see all his old photos and be happy. When the photos loaded and I saw the naked pictures he'd been sending to other women, I crumbled. Everything I'd known for so long was true, and in an instant, he'd shattered my whole world, and he wasn't even in the country.

It's hard to describe in words the absolute physical pain I felt when I found those photos on his memory card. I clutched at my heart and could feel it shatter into a million pieces. I was so angry at him, but more than that, I was just so *sad*. The horrible thing was that because he'd been away, I missed him so much and I just wanted to hug him and kiss him and hold him, but at the same time I wanted to hurt him, to punch him, to watch him shatter just like I had in that one second. He ruined every belief I had in him, every hope that my worst fears were just fears, every happy memory we shared which was now tainted by thoughts of him messaging other women. He destroyed my heart and everything with it.

You're probably wondering why on earth I then stayed with him for a further three years and the very simple answer is that I was still in love with him. The day before I decided to do this brilliant phone gift, I peed on a little white stick and found a faint pink line of joy. The day after I found the photos, Frankie came home, and I bled into the toilet and lost the only bit of hope I had left. These were two of the most painful days of my life, not including Grandad and Dad's death, and the traumatic birth I experienced. The problem was that these two days were one after the other. I discovered I might possibly be pregnant and was overcome by happiness, hope and love. I then found pictures of my naked husband and messages to women that were not his wife, and my soul died. The next day my period began and my potential runner bean baby slipped away. Three days of such raw heavy emotion and I remember leaving him a voicemail saying I'd found the photos, but I didn't care, I just wanted him to come home.

Of course, when he came home, we argued, I cried, I fell to the floor, and eventually after hours of tears, we both rolled into bed and I let him hold me. Not long after, after lots of thinking, I decided to forgive him and I thought once I'd made that decision, things would get back to normal, and we'd be happy again. It turns out, although you can try to forgive, it's impossible to forget.

Trying to work our way out of such a deep hole was so difficult and it always felt like a constant battle between us. I'd have days of crying non stop then days of sending him massive text messages telling him what I needed from him to move forward, sending him photos of quotes about forgiveness and how I would try and let it go and put it behind me. In the end though, it never worked, and I could never forget the pain he'd caused me. Around Christmas time, so about two months later and a year after his proposal, we spent Christmas Day at home but I was obsessed with checking his phone, seeing who had messaged, wondering what messages were being sent to his Facebook account and constantly logging in to have a look. I realise how trapped he must have felt from my behaviour back then, because I just *couldn't* let him have any privacy. The trust had gone, and it would never come back again. I regret so much staying with him when we both knew that I would never be able to move on. I know how much stress I put him under, always asking who this girl was and why that girl had sent this, and him having to explain it's just a friend, you can have a look, there's nothing going on.

I think from then on, for the next three years we remained married, we both became tormenters of each other. I could never allow him the peace and privacy he needed (and of course deserved), and he could never gain my trust back and make the hurt go away. I couldn't move on from it and every time I tried, something would just happen to bring it all back up. By the time I was pregnant in 2017, things between us were dead inside. The spark we once had walking beside one another in the school corridor had long gone, and though he tried at times to make me feel loved, I knew however much I loved him, I could never trust him again. By May of 2017, I was seven months pregnant and studying a counselling course which I loved, and my birthday soon came around. We went for dinner with my family, and on the way back his phone pinged. The message was from the same 'bath time' girl as all those years earlier. Every happy memory I'd created in those few hours of being with my family and him were destroyed in seconds, and the realisation that I would bring a baby into this world with someone I couldn't trust, hit me hard.

I must go back though, to before I was pregnant with my little bundle of hope and joy, to before I even found out that the man I'd loved so fiercely betrayed me so deeply, to the months after he asked me to marry him, when my eating disorder appeared like a monster. It was as though It knew the time was coming to consume me whole again, and It had been waiting patiently for a couple of years. When we had started dating, Frankie made me so happy that my eating improved drastically. He started taking me out, buying me ice creams, making dinners for us every night. He knew about my disorder, but it didn't stop him from encouraging and making sure I was eating enough. Those first two years of our relationship I was probably the healthiest I've been with food, because I ate meals and for the most part, I stopped counting calories and trying to lose weight.

Around the time of that Christmas where he proposed, I had begun feeling worthless again and I knew that things weren't right between us. The problem was I was so in love with him, I didn't want to admit it and he so wanted and needed to be in a relationship that he didn't want to acknowledge it. The months after he proposed are a bit of a blur now, I was working in a Doctor's Surgery at the time and at first, I loved my job. My anxiety has meant that over the years, I've always quit my jobs after perhaps one day or one week, and I've never stuck them out. This job, as a receptionist, I stayed at for over a year (with a little break in between where I quit and then begged for my job back.) After a while of loving work, I started to feel low again. I didn't like myself anymore, and Frankie didn't make me feel good enough or like I was worth much. I guess I needed an outlet, and that came in the form of restriction.

I started having panic attacks about my shifts which would either be something like eight till one in the afternoon or one till six in the evening. It was winter, so the evenings were dark, and I hated finishing late and having to lock up. I didn't drive, I lived a bus journey away and I hated being out when it was dark (I still do.) I started to not want to go in to work, knowing I'd be so tired and worried, and getting to work every day became a real challenge. I knew I couldn't just quit like I had done so many times before, because Frankie always wanted me to be in work, and I guess I didn't feel I could just leave my job this time.

Then one day, something just clicked where I started eating twenty calorie crackers during the day and that was it. I'd have a bit of cheese or jam and sometimes an apple or a cereal bar, but I started counting calories again and freaking out if I went over a set number. I started seeing the scale get lower and lower and I felt in control again, so I carried on.

When Frankie proposed, I suppose I felt this sense of pressure, because I knew I had to organise the wedding, I knew what everybody wanted for my wedding, but nobody seemed to care about what *I* wanted. I didn't want big or fancy, I didn't want all my family there. I just wanted the people I love most in the world around me and a small, quiet, simple wedding. Frankie has a *very* large family, so we ended up with one hundred and twenty guests – not quite how I'd imagined it turning out. Everybody would be on at me all the time, what's the plan for this, why aren't you inviting so and so, why have you made it that time... It just went on and on and I couldn't control everything, and most of all, I couldn't *please* everyone.

In the end, I just wanted to escape from my life, and I didn't want anything anymore. I'd lost every bit of drive, motivation, passion for my life, and I just wanted to disappear. This feeling just kept coming and each time it came it got heavier and heavier and deeper and deeper and no one could see me screaming. Then one day at work I collapsed outside the toilets because I hadn't eaten all day and I was on the late shift. They phoned Frankie to pick me up and I think somewhere around this time, I decided to go and seek help from my doctor. I was referred to an outpatient facility specialising in eating disorders, but it was in a difficult location and Frankie was never happy to take me. I ended up getting my colleague from work to take me a few times and then I just gave up because I felt like a burden. I remember thinking to myself that Frankie didn't even want to help me get better so how was he going to take me in sickness and health for a whole lifetime?

Whilst also restricting my calorie intake, I decided one day it would be a good idea to take laxatives. When I went to the shop the next day before my shift to buy them, something inside me got a niggle of excitement and fear. That night after work I took one more than the recommended amount and the effect the next morning was amazing, I felt as light as a feather. From that moment on I was hooked.

I began taking this same amount of laxatives every night and because I wasn't eating much, I began to just lose water and although I knew it was doing nothing to help me to lose weight, the empty feeling I got from them was such a high. I was completely addicted to the feeling after they'd worked, of just feeling free and light and *empty*. I needed that feeling more and more so I started increasing the amount I took by adding an extra one every night. I knew I needed to stop but I couldn't bring myself to throw the packets away, so I just kept going, kept buying more and kept putting my body at extreme risk. When I finally got to outpatients, the consultant told me my laxative abuse had become dangerous.

Soon it was August and our wedding was fast approaching. My family and I weren't on good terms at the time, barely speaking, and I had found support in one of my colleagues, who became a sort of motherly figure during that time. She remains a good friend now, but at the time she was who I would go to when I needed to talk about Frankie, my eating disorder, my life. She'd help me carry on at work and she'd always be there if I needed her. The night before my wedding I stayed at her house with one of my best friends and then the morning was here, and it was time to get ready. I was so nervous because of so many reasons but mostly because I knew I had to walk down this aisle with one hundred and twenty faces staring at me and I thought I was so fat and hideous, and everybody would be laughing at me. My dress was exquisite, a lace bodice that went in at the waist and then flowed out, a silky-smooth breath of beauty. I wore my hair down with no veil and we tried to curl it but it wouldn't go how I liked. Walking down the aisle and all I wanted to see was Frankie's face as he saw me. I wanted his face to tell me I was beautiful and worthy and that it was all going to be OK but as I walked down the aisle, he didn't turn around. Inside I think I knew then that things were never going to be quite right, and I was never going to be good enough for him. The rest of the wedding is a bit fuzzy because it was just so full on and constant. I don't think I sat down the entire evening and the only things I really remember were Dad walking me down the aisle, Mum reaching out to take my flowers, a sign that things between us might be OK and wanting Aunty Lins' cheesecake so badly but not eating anything all evening because my eating disorder didn't take a holiday just because it was my wedding day.

For probably a few weeks after our wedding, things between us were magical again. We loved being 'Mr' and 'Mrs' and we felt more in love than ever before. We'd show our rings off proudly and I thought that he was mine now and because we were married, he'd always be faithful, and he'd always love me. I was wrong.

By the November, after I'd found out about Frankie and my health had reached a serious low, I decided to go off sick from work and I never went back. I couldn't face the fact that the practice manager had told all the doctors about my eating disorder, I couldn't face the fact that I knew the staff were talking about me behind my back, and I couldn't face the fact that whilst I was there, I just wanted to cry. Then it was Christmas and I'd decided that it would be a nice thing to buy him a holiday away for New Year so that we could start fresh and put it all behind us. I increased the two-thousand-pound loan I'd got out to pay for our wedding to four thousand, so I could pay for us to go on holiday. Four thousand pounds in debt and we were booked to go to Spain for New Year. When he opened his present, he was disappointed because he wanted to be home so he could get drunk with his friends. I was so hurt that he showed no thanks or excitement for the fact that I'd booked our first ever holiday together. We didn't have a honeymoon because we couldn't afford one, and I wanted this to be a week for us to be together and have some time rebuilding the trust he'd destroyed. Through every little incident like this, where he showed no joy, no excitement, no appreciation and no love for me, my spark left a little bit more, and slowly my depression started to creep back in till it was in full force.

When we came back from our holiday, a fresh new 2016 had begun and we decided we would move to a two-bedroom flat, so we had more space. It was just that we didn't have enough space and we were in such a small flat, I'd decided, as to why we argued constantly. Nothing to do with the fact our relationship was burning right in front of us, it must have been the flat. We'll move and it'll be better. I'll trust him again. I am still so in love with him, I can't leave him. We can get through this and it'll all be OK. So that's what we did. We moved to a bigger flat and tried to rebuild our broken roots.

For a little while, we were happy again in our new flat. Frankie had gone to the effort of painting the whole flat before we moved in as a surprise for me. He'd painted the kitchen red with white spots all over the walls because he knew how much I loved red spotty things. He'd painted the bedroom duck egg blue because he knew I loved the colour. He wanted to show me that he loved me and he was sorry and for a while, it worked. We were happier and he'd come home from work and cook us dinner in our little kitchen and we'd put the radio on and dance around and have a laugh again. I wasn't working and had been out of work for around three/four months. I had become depressed again, and the thought of working made me want to curl up into a ball. I had an intense urge to be at home *all the time* and I didn't want to ever leave the flat.

Frankie wanted me in work, and so the slight spark we'd managed to light soon fizzled and things became awkward and stressful again for us both. Every day he'd go to work and I'd stay in bed, tucked under my duvet, either asleep or watching films because I had no energy to get up and do anything and I didn't *want* to get up and do anything. I spent every moment wondering if he was talking to girls at work, wondering who he was flirting with, wondering whether he was even at work. My mind went to the most ridiculous places and then I'd cry, uncontrollably, because I'd remember how we were when we first met, and how hard I'd fallen for him, and how much I still loved him. I'd remember the adventures he'd take us on and how we'd go for walks and get lost, go for drives and end up an hour away from home, go for a drink in the pub and laugh till we forgot what time it was. I'd remember all the things that made us, *us,* and then I'd feel even lower thinking about how we had to force all those things now.

My depression had taken over my whole body and, on the days where my mind wasn't snowballing everything, I felt numb and empty and wanted to disappear. I didn't have anything or anyone to tie me to the world anymore except my little sister, Daisy, who I loved so much and didn't want to ever leave. I went to my new GP and asked for medication and was put back onto antidepressants. I'd been on so many different ones before, for my eating disorder, my anxiety, my depression, but I'd always stopped them, not feeling as though they'd made any difference. My new GP suggested ones I'd never tried before and I had to keep going back to see him every two weeks to 'check in.' He had to keep increasing the dose of my antidepressants till eventually I was on the maximum dose and I felt like I could just about manage to do things again. I spent a bit less time in bed and more time on the sofa, I started going up the road to the shops for little bits maybe three times a week. I started *living* just a little bit more every day.

The months slowly started going by and I could tell Frankie was annoyed and getting down about my constant need for checking his phone, needing to know where he was at what time, who he was talking to, and I completely understand his frustration. I know I was a nightmare to be around but at the time I genuinely couldn't help it. The arguments were becoming more frequent and more verbally abusive and we'd shout and I'd cry and eventually he'd leave or it would be around midnight and I'd call my best friend to come and get me and we'd go to the drive through McDonald's and get an ice cream. I started self-harming more regularly after we moved to the new flat, because I couldn't *bear* the pain I felt on the inside. It was more than I could cope with, and I needed to let the pain out. I didn't feel brave enough to end my life, although I thought about it every day, and Frankie's words and his anger towards me made me feel so small and so betrayed, that I just wanted to scream. I was screaming on the inside *all the time* and I started to frantically need to slice my skin so that the pain would stop, the screaming would stop, it would all STOP.

I decided the next thing I needed that would make everything OK again was a kitten. I had always wanted one and I was going to get one this time. I looked on Gumtree, found some for sale and sent the message. When Frankie came home from work I told him we were going to pick up a kitten and he wasn't sure about it, until later that evening, when we got our new fur baby home and she started playing with him and chasing his hand around the sofa. We named her 'Belle' for a few reasons – it means beautiful, and although totally biased, she is stunning. One of Frankie's favourite World War Two planes is called the Memphis Belle and lastly, at the time, my little sister Daisy's favourite Disney Princess was Belle from 'Beauty and the Beast' and so it seemed like the best name all round. As I type this, Belle has just jumped through the window to come and give me a cuddle and I couldn't love her more. She's now three years old and I'm so glad I made that decision to part with forty pounds and buy what was a saviour for me at that time.

Belle quickly became my new best friend. She'd sleep on the bed with me all day while I laid there wondering why I was alive. She'd welcome me when I came through the door after I'd been to the shops. She'd start doing little tricks for us, like tapping our hands with her paw when she wanted a treat. She very quickly became the thing that kept me going every day and I knew I couldn't die because I didn't want her to be left with Frankie.

Life continued in much the same way, and we muddled by, one argument at a time. We tried hard to spend time together, and he was forever taking me to the pub after work, and not understanding why I was tired when I didn't work and had been home all day. I felt bitter and cold towards him, because although I was still deeply in love with him, I couldn't put the betrayal behind me, and it annoyed me that I couldn't just move on and forget about it. I just wanted to stay at home and in bed and feel safe, but Frankie is a great lover of the outdoors and of being out and socialising which is the complete opposite to me. I tried going out, he tried staying in watching films with me, but in the end nothing really worked.

Then, in November of that year, 2016, I was pregnant. I knew the night before I took the test because I had extreme period pain but still no period. I had been too lazy to go and get the pill from my pharmacy because I didn't ever want to leave the house and because depression really does make you tired *all the time.* It's no excuse but there we go; I didn't buy the pill and there are consequences to every action! Fortunately for me, I was *thrilled* to find out I was pregnant. I'd wanted a baby for as long as I could remember and being a Mum was something I always knew I wanted. Around six that morning, I knew if I went for a wee and there was no blood, I must be pregnant. So, when seven o'clock came and Frankie left for work, I rushed to the toilet again to take the test. A very faint second line appeared on the stick and I knew there was a little bean growing inside me. I of course rang Frankie straight away to tell him, and he was shocked (not knowing I'd stopped taking the pill because I didn't want to admit my laziness to him). After the shock, he was happy (although he did later express frustration at me being pregnant now because he wanted another year to do all his hobbies before he was ready to become a Dad.) After I told him I messaged my two best friends and I desperately wanted to tell Mum but I knew I wanted to tell her in person so I waited until Frankie had finished work so we could go around. It was officially out there which meant it was real and it was happening. I felt a small ray of hope and joy that I hadn't felt in the longest time. Things would *be* OK now we had a little bean of our own growing inside me. Boy was I wrong. Again.

When I fell pregnant, everything changed. I suddenly had an urge to eat better and take care of myself. I stopped taking laxatives straight away and I stopped my anti-depressants too and didn't take any for the whole duration of my pregnancy. I didn't want to risk *anything* because I knew that this little baby was mine and that I needed him or her more than ever before.

The hardest part during my pregnancy was having to physically get bigger knowing I couldn't engage in any of the unhealthy behaviours I was so used to using as coping mechanisms. I couldn't just restrict my calories because I was anxious about weight gain. I couldn't just take a few laxatives to feel 'empty' and gain back control. I had to look after myself and my growing baby now and I couldn't hurt myself anymore. For the most part, I managed to cope well with this mentally but when my Dad died, everything became so much harder.

I *needed* an outlet, a way of being in control, a way of coping. I needed *my* way of coping and *my* way to grieve and I couldn't do anything about it. I couldn't starve or stick my fingers down my throat or pop some pills. I had to just sit with the painful heart wrenching feelings that his suicide brought and *deal* with it. I can't explain the physical and mental frustration and anxiety when you need to cope but you just can't do it because you're carrying life inside of you.

Pregnancy brought the hardest challenges I've ever had to face. Not engaging in disordered behaviours and learning to cope in other ways when Dad died, by trying to lean on my husband for support and care, whilst also allowing my body to grow and stretch, were the biggest battles I've ever had to face. My pregnancy diary that I kept throughout the nine months is included below because there are some things that you never want to forget about the way you felt whilst you grew the miracle of life inside you… and my baby was the best miracle of all.

12ᵗʰ November 2016

I've just found out I'm pregnant. Oh my goodness I'm so happy. I'm scared but so happy. There really is a little bean growing inside me. It's the size of a sesame seed now which is scary because it's just so small. I need to start eating healthy now and I think I'm due on the 12ᵗʰ of July 2017 and am five weeks and three days today. I had cramps on Thursday 10ᵗʰ around midnight that woke me up, but I thought it was just period pain. I had slight constipation also and I am feeling a bit sick but not too much. I have slightly aching boobs, which are sort of like period symptoms really.

14ᵗʰ November 2016

I spoke to the doctor this morning, but I don't feel as reassured as I'd like. I'm at risk of getting some disease from Belle's litter tray and I'm still worried about having flu two weeks ago and taking all the laxatives. I just pray that my little bean will hang on in there for us. My boobs were sore yesterday but seem OK today. I feel a bit sick still but haven't been sick and have had no other symptoms except my back, which is aching a lot. Aside from that, everything seems to be fine... I am pregnant right? I told Daisy yesterday and she's happy and now I can't wait to have this little bean! I've been eating well and yesterday I had a small bowl of strawberry crisp cereal with an apple and some pineapple for breakfast. For lunch I had beans on toast and a banana and for dinner I had salmon with mash potato, parsnips and carrots, followed by a yoghurt.

I've been craving lots of savoury foods already and my theory is that when you're pregnant you go the opposite way in cravings. I'm naturally a sweet toothed person, but the thought of eating any cheesecake or sweets is off putting at the moment.

22nd November 2016

Hi bean... You're officially a blueberry tomorrow. Sorry I haven't written in a while. I've been so tired with you growing away inside me. You've been good to me though, and aside from some aches and pains, I haven't had any other symptoms. I know in my heart that you're a girl but if you are a boy, that's cool too little dude. I just can't wait to meet you. Just seven months to go! I'm praying with everything I have that God will keep you safe inside me and help you grow and thrive into a beautiful little baby. Don't leave me bubba. I need you. You've changed my life already for the better and I can't wait to hold you close to me and tell you just how loved you are. I can't wait for all the happy memories to come from your beautiful presence. Keep safe in there and keep growing healthy and strong for Mummy. I love you my little bean.

7th December 2016

I'm nine weeks today. I can't believe a week on Monday and it'll be the first appointment and then after Christmas the first scan. It's the BEST feeling ever. I'm struggling a lot with all the weight gain but it's a small price to pay for having you inside of me, a beautiful little olive now. I'm so blessed to have you and I can't wait to meet you. Stay strong my little olive. Mummy loves you.

17th December 2016

Hi bean. You're now ten weeks and three days and my first appointment is Monday, finally, some things are starting to happen. I can't wait to meet you. First though, I just want to see you on that screen, your little heart beating strong and brave. I've been craving lots of salty carbohydrates though, and you're a naughty bean for making Mummy a fatty. I've been eating lots of chips and waffles, tea cakes, pancakes and potatoes… anything brown really!

19th December 2016

My first appointment went well today, and my midwife was lovely. She gave us lots of information and to my relief, I wasn't put in the overweight BMI/high risk category! Phew. Passed that by the skin of my teeth. Welcome overweight and obesity from now on. I've been referred to the Sunshine Midwife team who specialise in mental health which would be nice to get some additional support from them. I have to wait for the scan through the post then I will really start getting excited. I just want to see you on the screen little one. I'm eleven weeks in two days.

20th December 2016

Feeling very low today bean. I feel lost and alone. I don't feel he's with me or supporting me. He just tells me things are my fault. I made him mad, I'm to blame. He turns it around on him instead of focusing on comforting me. Is it wrong to want more than that? To want love and support? I just feel so lost. I wish you were here.

29th January 2017

It's been over a month and I'm sorry I haven't written in ages. Things have just been manic getting ready for you and organising things. Your room is now empty and ready to be converted from an office to your very own little room. We've seen you on the screen and you are just beautiful. All wriggly and happy in Mummy's tummy, you just stay that way. The next scan is on the 22nd February and I can't wait.

30th January 2017

Sorry about yesterday – Frankie came in and I haven't told him I'm writing all this stuff down for you little one. I saw the midwife today and she let me hear your little heart beating and it was so beautiful. You're really in there, growing big and strong and ready to soon meet the world. I don't like what you're doing to my body, but you are worth every single pound I gain. I love you already bubba.

13th February 2017

Hi bubs. There's not much to tell you except we painted your room yellow yesterday and I hope you like it. Mummy managed to get paint in places where it should have remained white and Daddy now has extra work to do, but it doesn't matter. All that matters is you have your own room, your own peaceful place where you can dream about the world. Belle is keeping watch for you and keeping it safe and cosy till you get here. I'm excited to see you on the screen again next week little one. Remember I love you.

14th March 2017

Hi, my beautiful little GIRL! That's right, you're a little girl and we're so excited to meet you now. I'm twenty-three weeks on Thursday (in two days) and you're growing big now, making Mummy look particularly large. I don't mind though, because I can feel you making little bubbles inside my belly, which is you doing little kicks in there. I can feel you and I am so in love with you. Mummy's been a bit sad lately because Grandad died and now you'll never get to meet him. But I told him all about you and how excited I was to have you growing inside me. He was excited to meet you too, but life just didn't keep him here long enough and he just couldn't hold on. Soon you'll be here, my little ray of love and sunshine. I thought I'd tell you the cravings you've given me, so you'll always know what you liked eating when you were inside my tummy. You really like me drinking strawberry milk and sometimes I drink a whole litre a day. You also think Chicken Mayo 99p burgers from McDonald's are super yummy and the chips too. You could eat those every day. You also really love red grapes at the moment and you're a little bit strange because you love the smell of a fresh flannel and Mummy can sniff it over and over again because it smells so tasty. I love you little Alissa-Rose.

11th April 2017

Hello, my sweet little girl. I am twenty-seven weeks on Thursday (today's Tuesday) and you are doing just fine. You're a little wriggly thing now, moving around in Mummy's tummy happily... Especially after I've eaten! I don't have anything to report, except I still love the smell of a fresh flannel or any fresh laundry. I really like ice lollies now and have a weird addiction to angel cake too... I'm hoping you'll be a little porky thing and take some of this weight away from me but not too much, you don't want to hurt poor Mummy as I'm pushing you out. I have another appointment with the midwife who's called Sam on the 24th April and I'll get to hear your beautiful little heart beating again then. Belle's been a bit cuddlier lately, so I think it's you she loves. Your Nanny GG has been busy knitting you lots of little things which are all very cute but one day you'll call them the embarrassing baby clothes you had to wear. Your Aunty Dorcas has made you two giant teddy bears instead of small teddy bears like Mummy asked for. I found you a small little elephant I think you're going to love though. Me and Daddy haven't got anything else for you yet. We don't need much though, just the basic stuff. I think we'll start stocking up on nappies very soon... Just three short months till you're here in my arms and I just can't wait to hold you and know that everything will be OK because you're here and you're safe. I love you.

29th April 2017

Hello my little girl. I've just been reading back through all my little entries and I can't believe how much you've grown inside me. It only feels like yesterday I was calling you a little bean and I'd just found out I was pregnant, and I already knew you were a girl, even then. I'm twenty-nine weeks now, thirty on Thursday (today is Saturday), and I can't wait to be in the thirties now. Then it'll just be ten weeks till I get to meet your gorgeous little face. I can't believe how much you've grown inside me and how much you've made me grow on the outside. I shouldn't have been complaining all those months ago about weight gain because I look humungous now. I've just started to get stretch marks, thank you very much and I've stopped drinking strawberry milk now, but I still love angel cake and Maccy D's. I could inhale fresh flannels and fresh laundry all day long, even though it makes my throat feel funny and I still love crisps, especially when Daddy puts vinegar on the salt crisps. Your room is ready now and I have everything I need. I've got you a red spotty changing mat because that's just a little bit of me for you. You've got lots and lots of clothes – more than Mummy! Daddy still hasn't painted your elephant on the wall, but he's done such a good job on the rest of the room, so we'll let him off. Nanny Ray-Ray doesn't like her name anymore, so we're trying to think of something else to call her and I think it'll just be Nanna. It's Daisy's birthday next Monday and I'm trying to find her a present – I can't believe one day I'll be doing that for you my little girl.

I want to make sure you're safe. I want to make sure you know you're loved and cared for. I want you to always feel you can talk to me and Daddy, and that you grow up with good morals and values, manners and kindness. I want you to always follow your dreams, and I don't want you to ever be afraid or feel alone. Because you will NEVER be alone. No matter what happens in your life, I will <u>always</u> be here for you. I love you. See you soon my girl.

8th May 2017

Well my darling Alissa-Rose, today is Daisy's birthday and she had a dinosaur themed party this weekend just gone, and I felt huge. I love you so much, but you've made me grow uncomfortably large now and I no longer enjoy lugging you around. You're making my back ache lots, but I know you're worth every ache and pain. The mental strain though is certainly hard now my not so little bean. I feel people staring at how large I am and they say I must be ready to pop, but I still have another two months to go. You must be a big baby, but I don't mind at all, just get here safely. I love you so much and feeling you inside me and cradling my swollen, stretch marked belly every evening are moments with you I'll never forget. See you soon beautiful baby.

25th May 2017

It's my birthday bean and I've almost finished my counselling course and I got to leave early today because we're going for dinner with Mum and Ashleigh and Daisy and it's going to be lovely…

*I had to write to you again little girl, I'm so sorry for all the tears this evening. I can't believe my perfect birthday dinner was ruined by your father, **<u>again.</u>** His phone went off on the way home darling* *and it was a message from a girl. A girl who has messaged in the past, and there's always been something between them going on, although I've never fully confirmed what. Anyway, my beautiful bean, I'm sorry for all my emotions. I had such a lovely evening, Mum and Ashleigh and Daisy were so lovely to me and bought me so many beautiful presents and then Frankie had to ruin my last birthday before you're here. He swears nothing is going on, but I've never trusted him since, and I don't know where we're going to end up. I never wanted to bring a baby into this world unless I was 100% sure that I'd be with the Dad forever. I thought your Daddy was my whole world but these last two years he's let me down so much. He's made my heart hurt in more ways than you'll ever know. Whatever happens though beautiful, you'll always have your Mummy and we will be best friends forever. I'll always keep you safe. I love you.*

10th June 2017

I'm so swollen sweetheart. You're making me hurt more and more now, and I just want you here. I'm so desperate to meet you, and so desperate to have normal sized feet again. They're so swollen, some days I can barely walk. My belly looks so strained all the time and it feels like you can't possibly stretch me out anymore. You're still staying nice and strong though my gorgeous girl, and I know you're going to be just fine now. We're so close to meeting, and the first moment I get to cradle you in my arms will be the best moment of my life.

21st June 2017

I've done my birth plan so please try to come smoothly for me, OK? I want a nice calming water birth with dimmed lights and soft music, I want Mum right next to me and I want you placed straight onto me as soon as you arrive. I want to feel as much as I can with a little help from gas and air and that's what I want! I hope that's not too much to ask. I'm really struggling now, but it's under a month till you're due and I'm SO excited to meet you!

14ᵗʰ July 2017

You're late bubba. You're not here yet and I'm starting to panic. As well as feeling ridiculously uncomfortable, I'm worried you're going to be too late. Mum goes on a cruise on the 22ⁿᵈ and I want her to be next to me. I need her there, but you might not be here by then. I don't know what I'll do if you're late. I don't want an induction and I don't want to be scared and not have Mum with me. I need her, and I hope that one day, you'll need me just as much.

20ᵗʰ July 2017

I'M HAVING CONTRACTIONS AND YOU'RE ON YOUR WAY! I've lost the mucus plug thing that you lose but my waters haven't gone but they're definitely contractions. Thank you darling. Thank you so much. I can't wait to meet you. See you soon beautiful Alissa-Rose. Always know that your Mummy loves you and will always be with you.

~

Alissa-Rose, who we all now just call Alissa, was born on Friday 21ˢᵗ July 2017 at five-fifty-two in the afternoon, weighing eight pounds and eight ounces. Her birth was the most physically traumatic thing I've ever gone through, after Dad's suicide being the most mentally traumatic, and my eating disorder being somewhere fuzzy in the middle. I started having contractions on the 20th in the late morning, and they were irregular and more like period pains. I remember messaging my Mum in excitement because I knew this was it, and I was so relieved she'd be there for the birth. I bounced and bounced on the birthing ball to try and get Alissa moving and make sure that this was labour. By the late afternoon, the contractions were closer together and more intense. I had to lie on the sofa and not move to be able to cope with the pain. When Frankie came home from work around five, things were happening and then at some point we made our first trip to the birthing centre we were planning on having Alissa at. They told us I was only one centimetre dilated and to go home and take a bath and try and relax. I can't really remember much after that because the pain was obviously frequent and strong, but I remember I didn't want to get out the bath and then somehow we were back at the birthing centre but were told we needed to go to the hospital that was a thirty minute drive away to give birth and get pain relief. I still wasn't four centimetres so I couldn't have the gas and air and the birthing centre didn't provide any other drugs. When we arrived at the hospital I felt immediately better, the environment was calm and soothing and I was given pethidine and fell asleep for two hours around midnight. When I started waking up, I was so out of it I forgot I was pregnant, and then the contractions came again. The next hours are all a blur but Frankie messaged my Mum to come and as soon as she arrived, I felt instantly better. I had the gas and air, I was four centimetres, and I was in so much pain. I was being sick, and I needed a wee, but was too scared to go because I felt I might push the baby out. I went and my waters flooded into the toilet.

I was then rushed to a different room because Alissa had pooed in my waters and so I needed monitoring. I pushed for an hour and a half with no joy and so was taken to emergency theatre for forceps delivery. I wanted my Mum to come with me, but she let Frankie come and that's my biggest regret of all. I needed my Mum at my birth, and she couldn't be there. I know it's her biggest sadness about my birth too and although I love her dearly, I don't love her enough to ever have another one so she can be there! In the end, I didn't get my planned birth and it was probably the most horrendous experience I could have imagined. I was cut, I bled a little too much, and I was in labour for over twenty-four hours. She was worth every second though, then, now and always.

The day after she was born, my Mum was off on her cruise and so for the time she was away I was constantly in tears because she was the only person I wanted with me. I had many visitors, but thankfully no one came whilst I was in hospital. I couldn't get Alissa to breastfeed and I was in pain. I had a catheter in, I could hardly move, and I hadn't slept for goodness knows how many days. I was beyond exhausted mentally and physically and I remember the midwives just kept plonking Alissa on my chest and leaving me with her and I didn't feel safe. I wasn't looked after, and no one came to help me learn how to breastfeed and how to get Alissa to latch on to me. The next day, nothing was working, and they came to take my catheter out and pull the drip out my hand, which was bruised and swollen, and I just wanted to go home. I was bleeding, couldn't sit or stand and my legs and feet were so sore. We made the choice to buy formula milk so we could go home and once we were home things felt better.

The following few weeks of trying to breastfeed without much success, expressing to keep my flow going, formula feeding, and coping with a new baby were hard work. Feeding three ways was so draining and I could barely think straight. My healing was slow, and I bled for weeks after the six week 'healing' period was up. The night-time feedings were probably the worst because I couldn't lift her well and I couldn't get out of bed quick enough. We ended up putting her between us in the bed, and our co-sleeping journey began. Frankie would shout at her to stop crying in the middle of the night and this fuelled my bitter resentment towards him, and I'd cry at how disappointed I was by him and his behaviour towards our precious gift. When he'd go to work in the morning I'd be relieved that it was just us but also crippled with anxiety that I wouldn't be able to make her bottles fast enough because I couldn't get up or walk properly and I couldn't stand for long periods of time. Doing just the bare minimum of housework was too much for me and so I had to rely on Frankie to start taking care of the flat. For the first six weeks or so, he did the washing, the washing up, the cleaning and the tidying and was a rock of support. He'd make the bottles for me and he'd make sure I could get in the bath and wash myself. He'd just grab a quick hour nap for himself on the weekends so he could help out with Alissa during the day, even though he was tired from work and we were both up all night. People would comment on how fantastic he was and how lucky I was to have him and I did feel thankful towards him, but I couldn't shake the feeling I had of being so very let down by his night time behaviour towards Alissa. The feeling of betrayal kept building and building and everything was hard and painful, (and I don't just mean my boobs.) One day I realised that Alissa had what turned out to be thrush in her mouth. From then on, I knew she had a milk allergy and I felt an immense amount of guilt for not noticing sooner. The battle after that to get her on to special formula milk was horrific, and I felt like giving up so many times. Seeing her in such agony spurred me on to keep fighting and eventually it worked. We were given the most expensive, broken down formula and finally Alissa started sleeping better, had healthier nappies, and was more settled.

It seemed that everything was a constant battle, and the next hurdle that was thrown at us was Belle. Alissa started sneezing and I started scratching and scratching with sores appearing on my hands and arms where I'd been stroking Belle. I eventually paid out for private allergy testing which confirmed our fears – Alissa and I were allergic to Belle. It also confirmed Alissa was allergic to not just dairy, but egg, whole-wheat, gluten and some other foods. We then had the heart-breaking decision of what to do with Belle. I bought allergy medicines and sprays, but nothing was working so eventually we decided to rehome her. Fortunately, my best friends' sister and her boyfriend were kind enough to take Belle on and they looked after her so well for over a year till I was ready to have her back and me and Alissa weren't allergic to her anymore.

Everything kept being thrown at me, and it felt like a constant test to see just how much I could take before I buckled. Frankie, Dad, relapse, pregnancy, birth, Belle, breastfeeding, allergies – it went on and on and I felt like I couldn't breathe. I felt trapped and down and suddenly I felt like I was *never* going to get through this, and I was never going to be OK. My health visitor would come and each time she'd ask if I'd managed to make it to the baby groups. Each time the answer would be no because my anxiety had become something uncontrollable again, and I rarely left the house. I was afraid of *everything.* Of the pushchair getting stuck in the middle of the road, of Alissa screaming and me not being able to comfort her whilst out. Alissa doing a poo and not being able to change her, Alissa being hungry and not being able to feed her, people I know seeing me and seeing how *fat* I was and how disgusting I looked. The list of anxieties went on and on and I felt like things were spiralling out of control. My eating disorder took one glimpse and decided it was time to get back in charge and so the cycle of restriction, guilt, and relapse happened yet again.

Months into Alissa's little life and the only thing I was sure of was her and the intense love I felt for her. It was and is a love I've never known, so pure and so bright. It goes deeper than the deepest ocean and there is nothing I wouldn't do for her. She was my reason for staying with Frankie, my reason for putting on a happy face for other people, my reason for smiling when we'd go out for a drink to the pub after Frankie finished work, even though it was the last thing I wanted to do. The arguments with Frankie started up again after the initial loved up "we have a new beautiful baby" phase ended. He'd shout and tell me I'd never get custody of our baby because of my mental health, and I'd add a bit more resentment and hatred to my heart.

Eventually, after nine months and another house move, I decided to move to my Mum's. I was done and although I still loved Frankie deeply, I didn't think I was still *in love* with him anymore. I moved as much as I could into Mum's one day because I was absolutely sure I didn't want to go back to him but as the evening came, I was heartbroken and sad and he was the one person I needed. We'd agreed to give it a week and see how I felt at the end of the week and if I wanted to try again. I got to three days in and I knew I wasn't ready to leave because I still loved him too much. Whilst he was at work, I moved all my stuff back home without telling him, and then when he came after work at around five o'clock to see Alissa, I told him that I'd made a decision. He automatically assumed I'd chosen to leave him, and when I said no, I wanted to make it work and I'd moved my stuff back already, he said he wasn't ready for me to move back home yet, that there were still things he needed to do that week. That, along with finding a text from a female friend whilst sitting in the van and having him lie and fluster up excuses, made me realise that I needed to leave and never go back to him again. I was too tired to argue anymore and too tired to try. I went back for a while, I can't remember how long exactly, and then I packed all my things again and left. This time I didn't go back. When I left the second time, I logged into what was our joint Facebook account that same day, to see that he was already messaging other women and that hurt me deeply.

I lived at Mum's from March to September, Alissa and I sharing my little sisters' room and my little sister sleeping in my Mum's bed with her. Alissa would come into the single bed I was sleeping in and we'd stay next to each other all night long. She had never slept well and would be up most of the night crying and wanting cuddles and so the months at Mum's were physically draining and mentally exhausting, trying to put the pieces of my life back together. If I hadn't had Mum's support throughout that time, I'm not sure I would have made it back.

It took a long journey of self-love and healing to finally put the past behind me and let the hurt that Frankie caused me fade. I divorced him straight away, and he was happy to sign adultery as the reason for our divorce which was the one honest thing I think he ever did for me. He was with a new girlfriend almost straight away and somehow life just seemed to carry on. I found a little place for me and Alissa, and we're still here today, a year later. I healed from it all and me and Frankie are finally at an amicable place, where he allows me to be the lead parent and he knows how much I appreciate that, because it helps my anxiety to know that he listens to what I say is best for her… Afterall, Mum's know best!

Things with Frankie weren't all sad and hard. We had so many days where I looked up at the sky and felt such happiness because of him. He taught me so much, about all different things. Small things, like using a cross-headed screwdriver and how to cook pasta, to big things like what it really means to feel *in* love with someone. Frankie was and still is, the only person I have ever loved, ever had such an intense connection with. Before the harder days came and the suspicions and secrets came out, I had the best life with him. Although he treated me wrongly, his heart, I choose to believe, is still good. He is funny and quick witted, charming and very caring. He has a lot to give, and I hope that he has found his happiness because I have certainly found mine.

This lemon has been a hard one to write about because although I've healed from the hurt Frankie caused, it still sparks tears to my eyes. That only reminds me that I'm human and I have a good heart. I still feel the pain because I know how to *feel*. Real, raw emotions. I felt love for him with every fibre in my body and I'm not bitter about it anymore because at least I know how to love completely. I know how to love so much that I could never hurt that person. I know I can be trusted, and I know that I can love someone wholeheartedly.

I think the biggest lesson I've learnt from this stinky old lemon is that with Frankie, I became confident in the beginning, and I felt more alive than ever. He made my mental illness *so* much better, but my mental health only improved *because* of him and not because of me. I ate more, I left the house every day and went out at night, all because of him, and the person *he* is. I didn't do it for me. Therefore, when our relationship went sour, so did my mental health, and I relapsed heavily in my eating disorder, and I became afraid to leave the house and my anxiety told me I couldn't do things without him. What I've learnt from this is that my mental health could only ever improve if it was coming from *me.* The love and worth I have for myself had to come from the inside, and not from the love and attention that Frankie gave me. I gave *him* the power to determine whether I was happy, confident, sexy and free. That power was never his, and it took a long time to get it back.

Frankie, it's 2020 now and we finally seem to have found a space to 'be'. I've let all that's happened truly go and I'm so glad I have found this peace with you. We are friendly these days, and there is no bitterness between us. It's helped writing all this down, and I may have portrayed you as a bit of a mon-ster, because at the time of writing, that is how you felt to me. Now though, I can look back and remember our happy days with a grateful heart. You taught me so much about living and you gave me new experiences I will never forget. We weren't good for each other at the end, but for all those happy moments we shared together, I can now honestly say thank you. I loved you with my whole heart, and the day has finally come where I can say, *I forgive you.*

That leads me on to my next mould encrusted lemon, and how I went from being completely caged with my eating disorder, to now being quite free, most of the time.

Lemon Three

I've thought long and hard about how to introduce this lemon to you all, where to begin, what to start with, which area to cover first. This lemon is all about my mental health and it's probably my most challenging one to discuss because it's never ending, and a constant in my life. This is perhaps my mouldiest lemon, and over the years, I've kept many diaries, blogs and vlogs (which I'll type out because it's only 2019 and we're just not quite there yet with technology). I'm going to share them with you all, because this way, you'll get to experience my mental health, at the time that it's happened. This means what you read will be real and raw, with no sugar coating over this smelly lemon. It may not all be exactly in order, but you'll catch up as we go along. There's nothing else I want to say about this lemon before I share these entries with you except the first entry is the only one from 2006 for some reason. I think I kept it because it was my first birthday entry. The rest of that year's diary has been thrown so then we skip to the following year, and to keep it running smoothly, I'm starting 2007 with my next birthday. I don't want to give you my back story or explain what happened, because you'll just read about it as we go along. The diary entries from all those years ago may be a little scattered, because I didn't keep every single diary, so I've just pulled what I had. Time to cut this lemon open, and let the zest pour away.

May 2006 – Diary

Dear Diary,

Today was my first ever birthday and it was so much fun. At school, my form surprised me with a chocolate cake. PJ took me out of class, and we walked around the school and I just knew something was happening because it was all very strange. When we got back to class, everyone was sort of huddled together like penguins and then they all shouted, 'HAPPY BIRTHDAY' and sung to me. It was special. It felt a bit weird to have everyone focus on me because usually people don't take much notice of me in class. It was nice but kind of uncomfortable. I can't wait till I turn sixteen. Me and Lauren keep watching "My Sweet Sixteen" on TV and they all get such massive presents and parties thrown for them. They get cars and keys to flats and thousands of pounds spent on their parties. I know I won't get any of that, but it's exciting that I can now finally take part in these things and be just like everyone else. No more explaining why I can't celebrate my birthday and why I must sit out of assemblies. No more telling people that I'm a Jehovah's Witness and having them look at me as though I said something wrong. No more feeling out of place in school. I'm excited but also, I feel sort of lonely suddenly. I feel like all my friends from the congregation have suddenly just vanished and I don't have anyone now.

Anyway, today was a good day and we're having my very first birthday party on Saturday. It's going to be so much fun, Mum's doing party games and food and Lauren's coming and all my friends from my class will be there. I'm excited.

May 2007 – Diary

Dear Diary,

It's my fifteenth birthday and I'm going on a big boat with Ashleigh for her college prom. I'm excited because I'm wearing a pretty dress that reminds me a little bit of the dress

Rose wore in "Titanic". It's black with red sparkly bits scattered all over it and I love it. I can't wait to wear it and go and have a nice time. The thing is though Diary, I'm scared because I don't know any of Ashleigh's friends and I've never really spoken properly to any of them, they've always just been my big sisters' friends who come in the house and then leave again. I don't know what to say and I'm worried Ashleigh will just leave me and go off with them and smoke and get drunk. What will I do then? I'm scared about the food too, if I'm being completely honest. I told you last week that we watched this video didn't I, in P.E, and it was about that celeb who did some crazy diet. Well, I'm doing that diet now, even though I saw what it did to her and how grumpy it made her and how she didn't enjoy things anymore. I'm starting to feel a bit like that, Diary, a bit fed up really. I haven't been eating anything more than eight hundred calories a day, and I'm starting to want to eat less now. I want to just see how far I can go I suppose and see if I can lose maybe just a couple of stone. That shouldn't take too long should it? I've been losing a pound a day for the whole week I've been doing this now, and it's been great. I'm already half a stone lighter but I don't feel like that's good enough now. I want more, and I want quicker results. I suppose I'm just being impatient but maybe if I just restricted my calories a little bit more and dropped to five hundred, I'd be a bit lighter, a bit quicker. What do you think? I've had to start hiding you, Diary, underneath my mattress because I don't want my Mum to find you now I'm writing my weight down every day. I'm so excited Diary, to finally have something that's just mine and that I can do well. I'm not really enjoying school now and I feel like I've lost a bit of that enthusiasm I used to have when I came to school, to do well in my classes. Now I sort of care, but don't care. I remember being in Year 7 and straight away I read all the books in English, so I'd get my gold reading certificate. I did it within a week or two I think, and my teacher was so proud of me and I was always the top. I don't feel like the top anymore, I just feel somewhere in the middle, and I don't feel like I'm shining anymore. No one can *see* me Diary, no one can see who I am, and where I'm standing. So maybe if I just do this well, and get lighter, I'll be seen again, and I'll be the top again. Everyone is doing so much better than me in every subject and even Music and R.E I'm not the best at anymore. We're starting to prepare for G.C.S.E's and I'm really trying Diary, I really want to be the best, but I've become somewhat stupid in the last two years. I was so special once upon a time, every teachers' favourite and the friend you'd always come to for help. Now, I'm just nothing. I'm nothing.

May 2007 – Diary

Dear Diary,

I ate chips on the boat Diary, and I feel so upset. We've just got home, and I've weighed myself and I'm a whole pound heavier than I was this morning. I knew this would happen, why did I go, why did I let this happen? I was so strong today, Diary, I told Mum no birthday cake and I made sure I stayed at five hundred. I didn't go over five hundred. Now I must be at two thousand at *least* with those chips. I can't *believe* I allowed myself to eat them. I'm so ANGRY at myself Diary, I'm punching my stomach because it's _disgusting_ and I'm disgusting and I'm never going to WIN if I don't stay in control. WHY DID I LOSE CONTROL? I hate myself so much, I'm not eating tomorrow, I'm not eating a single thing. I HATE YOU.

May 2007 – Diary

Dear Diary,

I'm feeling positive today Diary. I know I can do this. It's already four o'clock and I haven't eaten anything yet. If I do this, it'll be my first day of fasting ever. I'm so excited! I hope I'm two pounds down tomorrow. School was OK, I felt a bit funny in Maths, and when I stood up, I felt dizzy, and I grabbed onto Julia's shoulder to stop myself from falling. It was a bit scary, but in a good way because it means I have control and I'm winning. It was so funny in Maths, Mr C bent over and his trousers ripped right down the middle. Everyone howled with laughter, but I did feel a bit sorry for him, he was so embarrassed he had to leave class and another teacher had to come in for the last ten minutes. If I ever become a teacher, I would probably never come back to school ever again if that happened to me. Mum's in a mood and so I'm hiding in my bedroom. I hate that me and Ashleigh share this stupid room. We've got a fake wall partition thing in the middle but it means Ashleigh gets the windows and I get the door half and she keeps trapesing through my room to get to hers with all her friends, with her music on loudly and smoking bongs out the window. Yuk. At least it's put me off eating anything. I feel so powerful. From now on, I think my daily limit should be five hundred, no more than eight hundred, and a good day is either a fasting day or up to three hundred. I can do that.

June 2007 – Diary

Dear Diary,

I'm cold and tired and I feel a bit rubbish to be honest, Diary, but Lauren showed me how to throw up today and it felt amazing. I'm so glad to have someone else to do this with. We can keep each other in check and push each other on every day. She's really good at making herself sick and I couldn't do it when we tried the first time but later on after she'd gone home, I ate some of my fifty calorie bread and felt gross, and I just wanted it out so I pushed and pushed and I did it! I feel so happy to have finally been able to do it and now I know that if I ever eat more than eight hundred, I can just get rid of it! We had a great afternoon eating ice cream, but then I felt rubbish because I couldn't get it up but now, I know how to do it right. Two fingers over the bathroom sink. It's so easy. Why haven't I done this before?

June 2007 – Diary

Dear Diary,

Me and Lauren have the house to ourselves tonight, tomorrow and tomorrow night. Mum's in Southampton at her boyfriend's house and Ashleigh's staying at her boyfriend's house too, so it'll be just us. We're going to walk home from school, go into Co-op, stock up on food and then come back and eat EVERYTHING. We're so excited! We're going to throw up and eat all evening long and it's going to be fab. I'm now officially just over a stone lighter and I'm so happy. I was listening to "Suddenly I See" today on my MP3 player and it made me feel so light and like I am almost light enough to float away from everything. I just need to lose maybe another three stone, and then I'll be *perfect.* School was boring and why do I have to have P.E as my last lesson on a Friday? So unfair. Me and Lauren have been to the gym every day this week after school, and yesterday I bought a cereal bar after we came out the gym from the Café, and I threw the cereal bar in the bin but I kept the rubbish so Mum would know I've eaten. She's been so great at just letting me get on with things, I don't think she's even really noticed that I've lost weight or stopped eating much. I'm glad we never really did the whole sit-down family meal thing. It makes it easier to just say I've eaten soup for dinner or toast or whatever. I did think about hiding my food in my room like Hannah from Hollyoaks, but I'm not sure Mum would even check. But it's a good idea for if I think she might start getting suspicious, I hadn't thought about it before. I'm so pleased Hannah has an eating disorder on Hollyoaks because I'm getting LOADS of tips. I don't have an eating disorder, I'm just dieting, but it's good to see what little things I might make use of.

June 2007 – Diary

Dear Diary,

I hate school so much. All the lessons are hard, and coursework is hard, and I don't understand anything anymore. I'm so stupid. Fat, ugly and stupid. Why do I have to have frizzy hair and be a fat hippo? Why do I have to be so tall and gigantic? It's not *fair*. I wish I was like little Soph, small and petit, everyone loves her. Lauren too, she's small, thin, a beautiful blonde with perfect curly hair, not like mine. Whenever we're out, all the boys look at her and it's fine because I don't even want a boyfriend, but I'm never going to get one at this rate, looking like this. I've started trying to straighten my hair, but as soon as I start walking to school, the air makes it go all frizzy and by the time I get to school, it's not straight anymore and it's not curly either, so it just looks awful. I need to start wearing makeup. I need to start looking better. Lauren made my school skirt shorter and tighter and now I just want to shrink, shrink, shrink until there's really nothing left of me. I hate everything at school, but I hate myself more. I hate that I'm fat. I hate that I'm just BIG. The *only* thing I've got going for me is that I have this control with food. I don't have a problem I'm just eating better. I'm going to get thin Diary, I'm going to keep going until I'm as light as a feather. I know I can do it.

July 2007 – Diary

Dear Diary,

Sorry I haven't written in a while Diary, everything is hard. Mum and Ashleigh are doing my head in, and I hate being at home. I looked on the computer yesterday at places to live in Surrey. I wish I could run away to Surrey and live there, just like when Julia Roberts ran away from her physco husband in "Sleeping With The Enemy". The man looks a bit like Dad in the wedding photo I have of him and Mum. I wish he wanted to see us more. I keep waiting for him at the kitchen window, for his van to appear, for him to spend Sundays with us. But he always cancels. He's always got a headache, he's always taking aspirin. He doesn't love us. Ashleigh scratched his face out of a photo of hers the other day. She didn't think I knew but I found it in her little box of things. Her with Mum and Dad but his face has been scratched away. I know she misses him too, but she'll never say so because she's such a tomboy. I hate that she smokes weed and goes out drinking and is so horrible to Mum but on the other hand I really envy her. She's so confident and loved by her friends, she's cool. I've never been cool. I wouldn't even know how to be. Our cousin, Emmie, who's also in my form class, she's SO cool and everyone loves her. She mixes with everyone and fits in everywhere at school. I don't understand why I'm so different. Why I'm so ugly and fat and stupid and why I don't fit in anywhere. I'm not cool, I'm not blonde and pretty, I'm not smart. I'm not such a loser that I get bullied. I'm just nothing, I fit in *nowhere*.

July 2007 – Diary

Dear Diary,

It's finally Friday and me and Lauren are getting cheesecake and a whole birthday cake for tonight. We're going to watch a film and drink wine and throw up and I can't wait. It's been such a long week, and I'm so hungry these days. I try not to be Diary, I don't *want* to feel hungry, but I get to History in the afternoon and I'm *starving*. I'm so hungry I can't concentrate on my lessons now. I don't even know what we're studying in History. I'm NOT going to pass my G.C.S.E's unless I work hard over the summer. I think I'm going to put you away for the holidays Diary, because then hopefully when I write to you again, when school starts at Year 11, I'll be at *least* another stone lighter, if not more. I know I can do it; I just need to STAY FOCUSED AND STAY IN CONTROL. I'm not going to give up and I'm not going to be fat for my last year of school. I don't ever want to be this fat again.

September 2007 – Diary

Dear Diary,

School's started and it's mid-September and I hate my life so much. I feel so sad all the time, but I don't know why. I almost want someone in the family to die, so I have a *reason* to be sad. That's such a horrible thing to say isn't it? But I don't understand why I feel like this. I've been cutting myself a lot Diary. I love the feeling of the small little sharp cuts I make with scissors. I love seeing the blood because it makes me feel alive. I love that when I've eaten too much and gone over my calories, I can cut myself and punish myself and hurt myself till I cry. I haven't failed with my calories much over the summer. I've mainly been eating two apples a day if I am having a good day, Weight Watchers soup and bread for dinner if I feel I *have* to eat, and sometimes I've eaten a cereal bar, which I know I shouldn't, but I can't seem to control myself. I'm so hideous. I look no better than I did before we broke up for summer, but my skirt is a bit looser now, and it looks better, I think.

I'm really pleased I have Mrs C, my form tutor, to talk to. Lauren doesn't have anyone except me. I can't tell Mrs C about my self-harming though, can I? She'd have to tell someone, and I don't want anyone to know. Mrs C knows all about my food stuff now, because me and Lauren sat in my garden one day and we were reading this magazine, and it had a checklist in it for eating disorders. The thing is Diary, we both ticked all the boxes. We both throw up in the week now, and always on the weekends after our binges. We both try and fast all the time or eat little. We both walk to school and back and go to the gym as much as possible. We both obsess about our weight and our bodies and we weigh ourselves every day. Lauren eats mostly steamed fish and veggies and I try not to eat anything at all. Lauren is very much obsessed with eating 'healthy' but as little as possible and I'm obsessed with eating low calories but whatever the food, if it's under my limit. We both agreed perhaps we needed some help, so we decided when school started, we'd go and talk to our form tutors. I spoke to Mrs C at the end of the day, and Lauren came into my class when she'd spoken to her teacher. Mrs C is so lovely and I'm so glad I told her everything, but she said she needed to tell someone, and I'm scared now. Lauren's teacher said she'd keep it confidential and that's not fair, I don't want my secrets found out but not Lauren's. Someone is going to tell Mum and I *don't* want her to know. I need to think of something to say, some way to make it sound like it's all a fuss over nothing but what can I do Diary? I need help.

Everything is suddenly tumbling further and further out of my control. I'm not ready yet to get help, why did I think I was? I'm still so FAT. I still need to lose so much. I need more time. It was stupid to tell Mrs C, although I'm glad I can talk to her now because she's just like family to me. I'll be so sad when school ends and I'll never see her again. I honestly don't know what I'll do without her.

September 2007 – Diary

Dear Diary,

I've tried to make light of it with Mum and tried to tell her I'm just on a diet and my teachers have gone over the top. I don't know if she believes me, but she's not said anything. We haven't had a chat or anything about it and she isn't trying to force me to eat so it's gone quite well, I think. I feel a bit like I'm walking on eggshells all the time, but I'm just happy I can still lose without her on my back. I've sort of got it just right really, no nagging from Mum at home and able to now talk to Mrs C at school. Finally, something is going in my favour.

October 2007 – Diary

Dear Diary,

It's Lauren's sixteenth birthday and we're going in a limo! I'm so excited! We're going to be driven around and then we're going for dinner. I'm scared about that bit but excited for the limo. Then Lauren's having a party and I have the perfect dress. It's a size ten Diary! I'm finally getting somewhere and I'm so much smaller now than I was. I'm nowhere near my ultimate goal weight yet, but I have met my goal weight one and two now and that's good. Lauren's Mum is so cool for letting us have a party and alcohol in her house. Mum would *never* let me do anything like that. I'm going to get ready now, bye Diary.

October 2007 – Diary

Dear Diary,

Lauren's party was so much fun, but I drank *so* much red wine. I can't even remember anything, but I remember being really drunk and going to throw up and Hannah followed me in and we had some sort of heart to heart in the toilet and she helped me get ready for bed maybe? I don't know, but I'm hoping she was too drunk to remember too. I think I may have told her I have an eating disorder. I mean, I wouldn't even say it's a *proper* eating disorder. I'm not underweight, not even close, and I'm not like super scared of food, I do still eat. I just don't eat as much as I did. Three hundred is a safe number and I don't think it's unhealthy. Whatever. The party was good, and it was nice to just feel a little bit free for once instead of pretending I'm such a good girl all the time. I hate being the good one. I hate that I'm the school prefect and that teachers expect me to do so well in my G.C.S.E's. I'm not going to get A*s, no way. Why have they even put that on my predicted results? I hate school. It's funny how I used to love it and love being every teachers' favourite. Now I hate it, but I still feel I have to pretend I'm perfect. I must be perfect. I'm pretending now, but I won't be forever. One day, I will *actually* be perfect. I won't keep failing. Why do I keep failing at everything? Like, I went for head girl, but Rachel got it, not me, and I just got prefect (not that I'm complaining Diary, because I'm Mrs C's prefect which means every day after school I can go and help her but we can chat about all this stuff). Why did I have to choose History and didn't get to choose R.E for my option? Why can't I shrink myself more? Why can't I cut myself deeper? Why do I just do pathetic little cuts? I'm such a failure, I can't do anything right anymore. Mum used to be so proud of me when I was in primary school, she used to write me little cards every time I got my school report, because it was so good, and she'd buy me a little present. Now I'm just nothing. No one.

December 2007 – Diary

Dear Diary,

Sorry I haven't written to you in so long. School is hard, home is hard, and I feel lonely. Me and Lauren are still doing well though, and we both love going to the gym. She goes on the bike and I run on the treadmill for an hour then we go and do weights. I don't have much energy these days, probably from the low-calorie limit. Maybe that's why I'm always cold and dizzy. Today in Music I couldn't get up from the floor. I don't know why? I just laid on the floor almost shaking, I think. It was as though I was in my body, but not in it at the same time.

The class started piling their coats on top of me and then suddenly I was in Mrs B's little Music office and she was telling me I needed to start eating more, and I don't know how she knows I'm not eating. I've never told her, so I assume the girls in the class told on me. She made me an Options hot chocolate. I drank it because I'm weak and pathetic and I was just so cold Diary. But I don't know which one it was. I don't know if she made it from a tub or if it was an individual sachet. If she made it from a tub Diary, who knows how many teaspoons she put in, and how many calories was in that hot chocolate. I'm meant to be fasting and I'm so upset, I just keep crying now I'm at home, because I *shouldn't* have drunk it. Why did I have to drink it? I'm such a FAT UGLY FAILURE. I hate myself more than anything in the world and I don't want to be here anymore. I don't want to exist. It's Christmas soon and I know I'll eat loads. I know I will. I'll binge and I'll binge, and I won't be able to throw up because everyone will be in the house. I don't know what to do anymore. I feel like I'm screaming on the inside, and no one can hear me. I need help but I don't want to stop. I can't stop until I'm at my goal weight. I'm not there yet, I'm so fat fat FAT. I need to just keep going, stay strong. *Nothing* tastes as good as thin feels. *Nothing* tastes as good as thin feels. *Nothing* tastes as good as thin feels. *Nothing* tastes as good as thin feels. *Nothing* tastes as good as thin feels.

December 2007 – Diary

Dear Diary,

Christmas was OK. I had to keep taking photos of myself to make sure my hip bones were still there, and my spine was still just poking through the skin. They are and I haven't gained. I'm so relieved, I thought for sure I'd be at least half a stone heavier but I'm not. I ate a lot of chocolate, but I did hide quite a bit of my dinner so maybe that balanced it out. I feel OK. Mum's going out for New Years' and I think Ashleigh too so I'll either be at Lauren's or she'll be here, and we'll drink and throw up. I can't wait, it feels like forever since I've seen her. We text everyday obviously, but I hate that my routine gets thrown out the window when it's school holidays. I really miss Mrs C. It's so strange not to have anyone to talk to after the day ends. She's like my anchor to this world, she keeps me alive and keeps me here, because I know I want to make her proud of me. She sees something in me, and I don't know what or why, but it's nice to have someone on my side. She means the absolute world to me and I don't ever want to lose her out of my life. When May comes and school is finally over, I know I'll cry, but I'll just be crying for her.

January 2008 – Diary

Dear Diary,

Today I was crying in the hallway with Lauren and the bell had rung but I couldn't move. I was so cold and tired and shaky and dizzy, and I just couldn't force myself to go to class. The thought of moving and going to History was something I couldn't face. We made it up the hall and to the Music office, where we found Mrs W. Mrs W is also very important to me, just like Mrs C. If I described them as family, I would say Mrs C is Mum and Mrs W is like your crazy Aunty who you have a close relationship with. Anyway, Mrs W knows all about my food stuff too and she's great. I talk to her a lot but not as much as Mrs C. Mrs W is a Music teacher, but not *my* music teacher. I don't even know how or why I started talking to

Mrs W really, she just appeared in my life and has stayed put. She's doing my G.C.S.E Music duet piano piece with me. We did it for my mock and I think I'm meant to choose a different piece, but to be honest, I can barely concentrate to play the notes so I think Mrs B is just going to have to accept that I will *not* be her A* student this year. Anyway, Mrs W was lovely as always and she wrote me a note for History, because I was late. I told her all about my self-harming and she was completely cool with it and I'm glad, because now I can talk to her about it and feel safe that she won't tell anyone. I know Mrs C cares too much and she would tell someone. I wish I could tell her about it because it's become such an important part of my life now. It's strange but I feel like I *need* to cut myself these days to just remind myself that I'm still here. Most days, I feel like I'm just floating around. I can't remember what has been said in each lesson, I can't remember even getting to school some days. Cutting sort of keeps me grounded to the Earth and I like the feeling. I like feeling something other than the sharp pain inside that won't seem to go away. I wish every night to fall asleep and not wake up, but every morning my alarm goes off and I get up to face another day of starving myself and hating everything about my existence.

January 2008 – Diary

Dear Diary,

Today in History I put my head on the table and couldn't pick it back up. Kelly kept trying to tell me to get up, but I couldn't seem to move my head off the desk. It felt so heavy. Mr M came over to ask if I was OK and I started crying. It's getting embarrassing now all these little things I can't seem to control at school. I cry for no reason, I'm tired, angry, cold, dizzy all the time. From the second I wake up to the second I go to sleep I picture dropping down dead and being free from it all. It's draining every part of my life and sucking every bit of energy I have in me. My head is constantly heavy and in pain and I am so tired, but I can never get to sleep at night. I lay awake for hours feeling my bones and panicking if I can't feel them digging into the bed. After class ended, Kelly ran into the toilets crying so I sent Mrs C in after her, to make sure she was OK. I think she had a go about me and told her about the History lesson. I don't really know why she's so upset about it though, it's got nothing to do with her. At lunchtime me and Lauren sat on the heater outside the P.E hall and talked about all the foods we wish we could eat, and what we'd buy on Friday for our weekend binge and sick session. I keep wondering if this pain inside my heart will ever go away, or if I'll live my whole life with this deep sadness that I can't get rid of. I've been thinking a lot about killing myself lately. I wish I could cut deeper, but the quick slices are all I can do. I fail at everything I do really don't I Diary?

January 2008 – Diary

Dear Diary,

Me and Lauren have started to inhale our deodorants and body sprays in the back of health class. It's so funny doing it in class because we try not to laugh and let on that we're sucking in our body spray cans. Today we sucked in a whole can of 'Charlie, Pink' and it felt *amazing*. We put our scarves over our mouths first, and then spray directly in. The hit is unreal Diary. It's so addictive, sort of like being drunk, but for a split second only, so you do it repeatedly to get a constant rush off it. I love it. I'm going through cans quickly though. Yesterday I did laxatives for the first time. Lauren does them all the time because she binges more than I do. I just like the feeling of not eating really. I thought I'd try them though because then I could just eat what I wanted yesterday and not worry about it. I took a swig of the syrup like Lauren said before school started and waited for what happened next. I'm so glad they worked in the evening and didn't work at school, how embarrassing would that have been Diary! I weighed myself this morning and I have lost FOUR POUNDS! I'm so chuffed. The thing is though, I don't like the feeling of not being in control, and not knowing *when* they're going to take effect. I'm not brave enough to do them again, but I'm so pleased I lost four pounds and I'm finally getting nearer to my ultimate goal weight. At least if I die, I won't die *fat*.

February 2008 – Diary

Dear Diary,

Tomorrow, me and Lauren are going to kill ourselves. I'm hoping that Mum will find you Diary, I'll leave you next to me. Maybe then she'll understand why I had to do this.

Mum – I'm sorry if I've made you feel sad in any way. That wasn't what I set out to do. I don't want to hurt anyone; I just want to be at peace Mum. I don't want to feel so low anymore. I'm so tired of feeling so sad all the time and I'm so fed up of still being fat, despite months and months of not eating much. It's probably not a big deal to you, and you probably don't think I should be so worried about it but I am. I'm worried all the time now and the voices in my head won't stop shouting at me. It's so hard to ignore them Mum, they just scream at me constantly to not eat and to hurt myself and to throw up and I don't want to do it anymore. I don't want to hurt anymore. I just want to be done. I want peace. Please tell Ashleigh and Jan I love them and Dad too. Can you give these letters to Mrs C, my form tutor, and she'll pass the one on to Mrs W for me? Thanks Mum. I know we've never talked about this but if I've annoyed you at all, I'm sorry. I'm sorry I couldn't be the best and get the right grades. I'm sorry I missed out on BSG by just a few marks. I'm sorry I'm a constant let down. Please forgive me and still love me. I love you SO much Mum. You'll always be my Mum, even if I'm moody and sulky, I still love you the most in the whole wide world. I just need to find my peace now. Love Leonie xxx

Mrs C – I don't know what to say really. Thank you so much for all you've done for me and for always being there at the start of my day and the end of my day, to chat with me and look after me. You're the one reason I've kept going so long, and the one reason I make it to the end of the day. You're family to me and you always will be and without you, I would have been so lost and alone and so much sadder than I am. I hope you know how much I love you and how important you are. You'll have many pupils and many prefects after I'm gone, I'm sure, but try not to forget about me and try to keep your cupboard tidy for me. Thank you for being *everything* when I just needed *something.* I'm so sorry for being such a burden all the time. Love Leonie xxx

Mrs W – I'm so glad I found you and had someone to chat to during the hard days at school. I'm so sorry if I ever took up too much of your time, I know how busy you are and how much everyone loves you. Thank you for always being there to do duets with me and keep me going in Music. Thank you for letting me offload all my problems and cry and hurt in front of you. I know you could have spent your time so much more wisely than spending it with me, so for all those moments that we chatted, I'll never forget them or thank you enough for them. Love Leonie xxx

OK, I think I'm ready now to leave this cruel world. It's taken so much from me and there's nothing more to take now. I don't have any energy left and I don't want to fight anymore. I don't want anything anymore. I just want to be dead.

February 2008 – Diary

Dear Diary,

Well that didn't go to plan. I didn't ever think I'd be writing to you again but here I am, another day, another entry. Here's how my suicide went. Me and Lauren went to Boscombe and got our latte and muffin and it didn't matter because it was for the last time and who cares if we gained a pound. We came back to mine and obviously no one was home, Mum and Ashleigh were both at their boyfriend's houses. Lauren brought over her pink fluffy blanket and we laid it on the lounge floor with all the paracetamol we were going to take. We got everything ready and we *were* ready to go. Then Lauren decided she needed a bit more time. She asked if we should really do this or if we should wait a while, maybe do it another day. I wanted to go, but I didn't want to go without her. I said let's phone somebody to say goodbye, maybe that would help. She phoned her boyfriend and I phoned Mrs C. I found her number in the Yellow Pages, and I'm sure now she'll think I'm completely crazy and pray I never bother her ever again. I told her what I was going to do, and I said goodbye and the next thing I knew, Mum was on her way home, the police were coming around and Lauren's Mum was furious and walking over. It all went a bit crazy from there and the police had to have a chat with us and Lauren's Mum whisked Lauren home and now I'm crying and cutting because I don't know if she'll ever let me and Lauren see each other again. I'm so sad. I just wanted to die in peace, why did it all have to go wrong. I don't want to go to school tomorrow. I'm scared to see Mrs C; she's going to be so angry with me. I didn't expect to be alive today and now I am, and I've got food inside me and I'm angry and I'm sad and I just want it all to END.

February 2008 – Diary

Dear Diary,

School was OK. When me and Lauren arrived, Mrs C who we don't like and Mrs C who we also don't like very much took us upstairs to the office and told us we needed to go and say sorry to my Mrs C and we were stupid and all sorts of horrible things about how we worried everyone. That wasn't what we wanted, we just wanted to be at peace why does nobody understand that? After they had finished telling us off, we went downstairs, and Lauren went off to class and I went to find my Mrs C. When I got to my form room no one was there but her and when I went in, she hugged me so very tightly I didn't think she'd let go. I thought she'd be so mad, but she was just so happy I was OK and alive. I didn't think anyone would really care if I was here or not, so it was weird for her to be so relieved to see me. I was so happy to see her, and I cried. She's the reason I'm alive and the reason I will stay alive. I don't want to hurt her again or let her down. She is the only reason I will try to get better. I think me and Lauren are going to get some proper help now. I think we've been referred to some young people's counselling or something. I hope it helps but I don't feel like anything will get rid of this screaming inside my head and this *need* to keep the control I have over food. I haven't eaten since Saturday evening when the police and Mum were round. I didn't want them to get suspicious, so I ate a tin of fifty calorie soup and a slice of fifty calorie bread. I didn't throw up afterwards and I'm annoyed about that, but I didn't eat all day yesterday and it's Monday today and I haven't eaten anything all day. I threw my toast that Mum thought I was having for breakfast in the bush on the walk to school and the apples in my bag I've thrown away too. I've told Mrs W I've eaten though. I don't like to lie to Mrs W and Mrs C because they mean the world to me, but I don't need anyone watching me right now. I need to just stay on track. If I can lose just one more stone, I think I'll be ready to stop.

February 2008 – Diary

Dear Diary,

I hate this eating disorder. I know I have a problem and I desperately want help, but I don't feel like I can stop. I don't want It to leave me. This voice inside my head is screaming at me *all* the time, and I don't know how to turn it off. It's screaming at me *all the time* one hundred, one fifty, three hundred. Stop you fat cow, no more, you'll be fat, you'll be disgusting. What do you mean, will be, you already *are*. You could have so easily not eaten today, you had it girl, why did you eat? What possessed you, you weak PIG! You could have controlled yourself so much better today. Right, that's it, no more, you're not eating for the rest of the day. In fact, as of now, you pathetic fat slag, you can fast, for the rest of the week. But... I can't... I'm not prepared, I need time.... I can.... I will.... I'm sorry, I didn't mean to. I am weak, but I'll be better, I promise. Don't leave me, I'll be strong, I can do this. I won't eat, I'll show you. Just black coffee. I promise. Till Friday... Why do you haunt me? Why didn't I just stop that stupid diet? That stupid diet. I'm screaming inside, I can't cope, I can't breathe. Just STOP. Stop, I can't take it anymore. Leave me alone, please, I can't do this anymore. Help, I need help. I can't keep doing this, I need to be free. I need peace. I need to die. I want to die. I just want to be gone, so I can't hear you anymore. You're evil, I'm not fat, I'm not fat. I'M NOT FAT.... No, I didn't mean that, I'm sorry, you're not evil, you're a friend. A good friend and if it wasn't for you, I'd be fat, I am fat I mean. I love you. You keep me strong. I have control because of you. I'm sorry, please don't go, I do need you. Please, help me. Look, I've got the elastic band on and every time I think of food, I promise I'll ping it as hard as I can. I won't eat. I mean it this time. I'm sorry. Cow, you don't deserve to be here, slice yourself, go on, I know you want to, just do it. That's it, one more, come on, make them even. Nice little cuts all up your arm. Better do your leg too, you don't want anyone seeing them. Make the pain go away, make *me* go away. You're right, you can't. I'm here and I'm staying. You're fat and you're pathetic but I'll help you. I can help you. I'll make you thin. You love your bones, right? You know your hips don't stick out that much, the mirror plays tricks on you. They're hardly even there. Don't even get me started on your collar bones. That gap in your thighs could be so much bigger. You think your wrists are small but they're not. As for your face, well, I can't bear that people even have to look at you. Where's your jaw line? Where's your control? You let me down today. You could be so much better. Let me help. Stop now, you've cut enough, you don't need to keep going. That's too deep. STOP.

March 2008 – Diary

Dear Diary,

Today and last Tuesday I've had to go to the school nurse. I haven't told her I self-harm or anything. I'm not sure I like her, and I didn't even know we had a nurse type counsellor that worked in the school. It means I get out of a bit of History though one Tuesday and then a bit of P.E the other Tuesday which is great. I hate Tuesdays because it's double History then double P.E or the other way around and they're my worst two subjects. Mr M keeps asking if I'm OK and I say yes but I have no idea what we're learning about. Queen Mary and Mary I and they're different but I can't keep track of who is who and who did what and why I need to care. The potato famine was easier than this. I'm failing at everything. My school counsellor is OK but wants me to keep a food diary which is stupid because I'm just going to lie about what I'm eating obviously. I can't just write down black coffee or apples and a Weight Watchers yoghurt, can I? This is all so stupid. I just wanted it to be me and Mrs C, and just talk to her at the end of the day, without all these other people getting involved. They all want me to stop and I do too because the voice is getting louder and I feel so awful all the time. I'm horrible to Mum now, everything she does is wrong, and I want to say sorry, but I can't. I want her to give me a hug, but she never does. She doesn't talk about what's going on and I need her to. I can't just say things out loud, I need her to ask me, to hug me, to let me cry. But she never does. Ashleigh's always been her favourite, I'm just the crap youngest child. I don't even want to do piano lessons anymore and I love music. I just don't care about anything. I cut deep today. Deeper than usual. It hurt a lot and bled for a long time. I thought maybe I'd need proper help, but it stopped eventually, and I think it'll be OK. I never wear short tops or anything so that's fine. I've got Mufti Day coming up soon and I really want to wear this mini skirt I bought with Lauren and it's a size eight and I'm too scared to try it on but I'm going to. It's my goal skirt and I *must* get in it for mufti. We've got the rest of this week and then next week and then it's the week after so from Monday, me and Lauren are fasting *all* week or just eating two pieces of fruit if we feel we really need it. We can do this. I want to lose seven pounds in the week. I know I can do it if I just stay strong. Stay strong, think thin. Stay strong, think thin. Stay strong, think thin. Stay strong, think thin. Stay strong, think thin. Stay strong, think thin. Stay strong, think thin. Stay strong, think thin.

March 2008 – Diary

Dear Diary,

It's Monday and so far, no food has entered my mouth, yay. I've had a cup of black coffee with two sweeteners (four calories) but I'm not counting the sweetener unless I have more than three cups of coffee and go over ten cals. School was boring as usual, but I helped Mrs C tidy her cupboard again today and got all the books neatly piled and we had a good chat about stuff. She's literally all I have in the world aside from Lauren. Lauren's gone home to get her sleeping stuff and then she's coming over and sleeping here all week so we can fast together. We're better when we're together because we don't slip up. I weighed myself this morning and I'm two pounds down which is OK. I was hoping for more, but it means I have five pounds till this week's goal is met. I'm trying the skirt on Friday and am praying it'll fit me. Either way it'll give me the motivation to *not* binge Friday and Saturday night with Lauren. I'll either be too fat to wear it and need to still fast to try and fit in it by Monday or it'll fit, and I'll have to just go a little bit lower so it's comfortable. I *will* get into this skirt by next Monday. I have to. I can't be fat anymore. I don't *want* to be the fat friend anymore. I want to be the skinny one, so light I could just drift away. I want *no* fat to cover my five-foot ten beast frame. I look a bit like the beast from "Beauty and The Beast" and I would much rather look like Belle, Diary. OK, I'm going to set up the lounge ready for Lauren. I'll write again when I can. Wish us luck!

March 2008 – Diary

Dear Diary,

THE SKIRT FITS DIARY!!!!! I'm SO happy it fits! It's Monday now and I'm six pounds lighter. I'm so annoyed that I didn't reach the full seven pounds this week and I know it's because on Wednesday, Lauren went home for a bath and I ate a cereal bar. It was ninety cals and I shouldn't have eaten it. I failed my fast. I didn't tell Lauren Diary, I didn't want her to know how completely useless I am. Pathetic. Fat. Ugly. Useless. FAILURE. I'm trying to just forget about it to be honest because I cut all up my arms and legs after I'd eaten the cereal bar and it stung so much and my clothes stuck to the blood. It doesn't matter, it doesn't matter, it doesn't matter. It's

Monday, I'm one pound away from target and the skirt fits. I can wear the skirt on Thursday for Mufti, and it'll fit, and I'll officially be a size eight. I've always dreamed of being a size eight and finally I'm there. I'm still fat, but at least I'm getting somewhere. Lauren is a size four to six now. She's the smallest I've ever seen her and I'm so jealous. My hip bones and collar bones stick out lots, but her ribs and her spine really poke through the skin and I so wish mine did too. She has a drawer in her bedroom filled with cereal bars and binge foods and I wonder how she doesn't eat everything the day she buys it. I don't have a drawer because I have no self-control. I'm useless and pathetic. I'm going to wear my silver vest and black chunky cardigan with my mini skirt for Mufti. I just hope I don't look gross. I want to just, for once Diary, look *skinny*.

March 2008 – Diary

Dear Diary,

It was Mufti Day today and I wore the outfit I'd planned with some knee high boots and I felt like I was finally almost at my goal weight. I could see my hips poke out through my skirt and I love the feeling so much. I didn't feel well today though Diary, I thought I might faint a few times. Fasting is such a rush! I love it so much, but it really makes me feel weak and cold and bruised and shaky all day long. I don't have a clue what lessons I had today and what went on around me. I felt completely numb today, as though the floor had opened up into a black hole and I was being sucked underneath it and I just wanted to fall in because I was so tired and cold and dizzy but I had to keep going. I don't want to keep going Diary. I don't want to keep trying. I want to lose just another stone and then I can die *thin*.

April 2008 – Diary

Dear Diary,

Another month over and I'm still alive. I want this disorder to be the reason I die. I want it to kill me. I don't have anything interesting to tell you, life is rubbish and boring. Me and Lauren keep walking round the roads with our music on just for something to do to stop us thinking about or eating any food. My food diary that I keep for the counsellor is full of lies. Some days I try to be honest about what I've eaten but I never manage to leave it at honesty, I always add a lie in. During the week I make sure to stay under three hundred cals and no more than five hundred because that is repulsive. I always lie about breakfast because I think if she ever challenged it and asked Mum, Mum would agree that I 'eat' breakfast because she smells the toast and I take some crumbs from the bottom of the toaster and sprinkle them on my plate and then throw the toast in the bush on my way to school. I always put something down for lunch, usually fruit and sometimes I lie and put down a tuna lunch pot thing (two hundred and fifty) which I've only actually eaten once at home for dinner. I don't eat dinner, so I tell the truth in my food diary and put nothing. What she sees when she looks at my food diary is something like this;

Monday to Friday: Toast for breakfast, two apples and a cereal bar for lunch and nothing for dinner.

Saturday and Sunday: Cereal for breakfast, a latte and muffin for lunch with Lauren and nothing for dinner.

That way, she feels like she's helping me when she sees my diary and she thinks there's room for progress but I'm at least eating *something*. What I have <u>*actually*</u> eaten for the last three weeks is this.

Monday to Friday: Black coffee for breakfast, an apple for lunch and an Options hot chocolate and tin of Weight Watchers soup for dinner, except on Friday night, which is a binge evening with Lauren.

Saturday and Sunday: Black coffee again for breakfast, a latte and muffin for lunch with Lauren and an evening binge Saturday evening with Lauren followed by nothing for dinner on Sunday.

It's very nearly *almost* the same isn't it? The thing is Diary, I don't want to tell her about the binges because I'm so ashamed of myself and feel so guilty. I eat SO much with Lauren on Friday and Saturday evenings and of course we throw up, but I've still eaten it because I'm a fat pig with no willpower. I can't tell her how much I eat, it's disgusting. No wonder I'm so horribly fat. I'm almost underweight on the BMI scale and I just don't *see* it. Where has this weight gone, where have I lost it. I'm still so *FAT*.

April 2008 – Diary

Dear Diary,

It's one month till my birthday and I'm freaking out. School is nearly finished, I don't want to say goodbye to Mrs C and Mrs W, but Mrs C more. I've got exams coming up and it's my sixteenth and Mum wants to go for a meal. I can't go for a meal, I can't, I'll get fat. I'm only *just* near my goal weight. I can't stop now, I can't fail. I'm not going to get my G.C.S.E's and I can't fail in anything else. I'm worried about History and Maths the most. I used to be good at Maths and I used to *love* History but now they've become my worst nightmare. I hate everything about them. I hate school, I hate walking down the corridor and knowing everyone is watching me, wondering why I don't just disappear. Wondering why there's a fat monster at school. I hate being so big, even though I do like being in Year 11 and being the oldest. We've got Muck Up Day and ROA day in May (which is like the leavers assembly and we have to dress nicely), so I need to fast to make sure I look my best. Then, in June we have Prom and I *need* to find the perfect dress. Mum doesn't want to spend much money though on a dress so I'm going to look hideous. Everyone else is getting pretty dresses and I'll probably go looking like 'Shrek'. Life is poo.

May 2008 – Diary

Dear Diary,

I haven't written in ages because things have been busy. My form class went out for a meal with Mrs C and it was an Italian place so everyone had a pizza but I chose a tuna salad to be on the safe side and when it came out it was bigger than all the pizzas, it was massive! I was *so* embarrassed; everyone was looking at me and I bet they were thinking what a fat cow for eating so much. I went to the toilet to throw up after, but I couldn't because some girls followed me in. I threw it up when I got home but I didn't get it all up so I know I must have had at *least* three hundred cals. It was nice to be *out* though, and I got to sit next to Mrs C with Kelly on my other side so that was nice. It *sort* of made me see that things aren't always sad and miserable, like everyone in my class was so happy and excited to almost be finishing school and going to college. It made me think a bit that maybe I *could* just live and see if things get better. Maybe I can be happy *and* have my eating disorder. I just wish it would go back to how it was at the beginning when I felt so light and in control and *free*. Now I sort of feel a bit trapped Diary, but my eating disorder is screaming at me not to tell you. But I do. I feel trapped.

May 2008 – Diary

Dear Diary,

It's Muck Up Day tomorrow and I've not eaten for four days except one day in the middle where I ate one Weight Watchers yoghurt (fifty-four). I've got my outfit sorted, I'm going to be 'Runaway Bride' and wear Mum's wedding dress and trainers. I'm super excited. I feel weak though and all dizzy and cold again. It's worse when I've not eaten. I'm just trying to stay focused on my goals. I *want* to look good, so I *have* to fast. It's the only way I'll get to my goal weight and the only way I'll win and not fail. I *have* to stay strong.

May 2008 – Diary

Dear Diary,

Muck Up Day was fun but me and Lauren both felt so ill. I've decided Diary, that I think it's time to stop now. I'm not at my new ultimate goal weight but I've had enough of feeling so rubbish all the time. I hate feeling so cold and tired and dizzy and sick and I hate that this is ALL I think about. I want to think about other things. Everyone was having so much fun yesterday and laughing and taking photos in their outfits and me and Lauren were just trying to stay alive really. I want to be happy too, I want to laugh and enjoy things. I don't want to be this way anymore. The eating disorder is shouting at me and making me feel bad and making me pinch myself and hurt myself, but I don't want to anymore. I want to change. I'm going to eat something for dinner. I am Diary, I want to be alive again.

May 2008 – Diary

Dear Diary,

I've been eating a bit more, but *It* still won't shut up. I'm scared of getting fat and my brain is yelling at me that I'm just getting fatter and fatter. I don't want to be fat at prom so maybe I'll just restrict till prom and *then* I'll start eating more. I don't know what to do or where to start or how to get better. I'm applying to sixth form and I don't even know if it's what I want to do. I can't think straight anymore. Everything is so hard. ROA day is coming up, it's like an assembly where they say goodbye to all the Year 11's and give out certificates and stuff. Mrs C has to say something about our form and I'm hoping she'll mention me even though I also don't want anyone to focus on me. I don't want to say goodbye to her, I can't think about it without crying. She's my whole world, what will I do when I leave, who will I talk to?

June 2008 – Diary

Dear Diary,

It's prom tomorrow and my dress is here, and I don't like it but it's too late to do anything about it. Leaving school was hard. ROA day was awful, I cried because I didn't want to leave Mrs C, but everyone else was crying because they didn't want to leave their friends. Me and Lauren live three roads away, so I'll see her all the time still. But Mrs C and Mrs W I won't see anymore, and I miss them both so much already, and it's only been a couple of weeks. Sorry I haven't written, I've been sort of eating more, but gaining weight and then freaking out and then restricting again and now I'm in a stupid eating then fasting sort of routine. The last three days though I've fasted, so I look my best for prom. I'm still going to look fat, but hopefully I won't look *as* fat. I washed my hair today ready for tomorrow, but I could hardly stand up. I used to be able to fast so easily, now it's so hard to not eat. I hate my stupid fat body, I'm so weak and pathetic, I used to have so much control. I just want to be *normal*. I feel like I'm screaming inside, and I can't get out, I just want to rip my chest apart and jump out of this horrible disgusting body. I don't even want to go to prom, what's the point. But I'll see Mrs C and that'll be the best thing ever.

June 2008 – Diary

Dear Diary,

Prom was fun but I looked horrendous. I took my hair out of the clip at some point during the evening and I didn't realise my hair had puffed up about five times and was all frizzy! How embarrassing. I bet Mrs C wondered why she bothered saving me. I'm a horrific mess. Anyway, now all the important school events are over I can breathe a bit easier. I can just hide away in my room for a while and that will be nice. Me and Lauren are going to Costa for a muffin and latte. I'm tired and Lauren's hungover. She tried to flirt with the male teachers she fancies at prom, it was so funny. Everyone was in these long princess type dresses and Lauren walked in wearing a short animal print dress! I love her so much. She's the *best*, best friend in the world. Well, I'll write soon Diary, there's not much else to say now school is finished.

July 2008 – Diary

Dear Diary,

Me and Lauren have already talked about going back to school to see Mrs C and Mrs W when school starts in September. I don't want to go to sixth form but it's too late now. Lauren's going to college to do beauty and I really wish I'd chosen the same college too, but I didn't really know what to pick and now I don't even want to do any of the A Levels I've chosen. The only slightly good thing is that Mrs W goes to that college some days to teach Music so I *might* see her. So far things have been boring, and I don't have anything to tell you. Being at home with Mum and Ashleigh is annoying so I mostly just stay in my room or go to the gym. I've been trying to eat better but I just keep getting freaked out about the scales going up so then I just restrict back down again. My head is always busy and always shouting at me and telling me off for one thing or another. I can't seem to do anything right really. I'm a rubbish daughter, the fat friend, not cool, I don't drink or smoke, haven't had sex like everyone else. I'm just a bit useless really Diary.

I'm running out of pages now, so I think I'll start a new Diary in September when sixth form starts and maybe then, I'll have something happy to tell you. Maybe one day you'll be famous like Anne Frank's 'Kitty' – but my life is poo, so I doubt it. OK, bye Diary.

~

July 2018 – Blog

This is my first ever post, and I'm feeling nervous and excited
about finally being able to connect with you all, share my
experiences with you all, and have a place that I can talk and
you can read.

Today has been a stressful day, and I'm going to keep it short
because I'm very tired. I thought my flat, which is currently
being worked on, would be ready by tomorrow and I'd be
moving this weekend, but it turns out it'll be another week
before it's ready. Does anybody else find that when stressful
situations occur, their mental health takes a tumble? I could
literally *feel* my depression seeping in, and I'm just like, 'no
thank you depression, go away and take a nap.' I know the
situation isn't that bad, but the mentally ill me is screaming
that everything is going wrong, you are a failure, nothing is
going to work out and you will forever be stuck here, feeling
like this. Almost like the mentally ill part of my brain is
laughing at me, because It knows that It has an opportunity
to sneak in and cause destruction. Leonie xox

July 2018 - Blog

It's Friday 27th July 2018 and after many attempts this
morning to write to you, I have finally sat down. Here's a bit
about *me*. I'm a twenty-six-year-old, single mother, recently
divorced and currently living back at my Mum's house. I
want to start a blog so I can talk freely about all the things that
fill my mind day and night, and so I can offload my worries
with you all. I want to talk about what being twenty-six and
going through a divorce is like and how it has impacted my
mental health. I want to talk about when I first developed my

eating disorder and what the triggers were. I want to talk about everyday things, like, how do I manage having a one year old and mental illnesses? How did my eating disorder, depression and anxiety affect my marriage and relationship with my now ex-husband? Do I have support within my family? These are all things that I think are important to get out, because they're all the things that build up in my mind and cause further triggers for me. I want to write because I know I am NOT alone. We are all in this together and we must make the choice, every day to give recovery our best efforts. It's not easy, it never will be, but living even partially recovered, is one hundred times better than living in the darkness of mental illness. I choose recovery every day in my own way, because I am choosing to *live*. I'm choosing to fight a bit harder, work harder, be happier, make better choices. I am still struggling with all my mental illnesses. They have not gone away. But I really believe that if we have the strength and courage to ignore their booming voices, then every day we can get stronger, and to me, *that* is what recovery is all about. Leonie xox

August 2018 – Blog

I do NOT like what I see when I look in the mirror. I hate my gestures and facial expressions, the bags underneath my eyes, the way my jawline has slowly disappeared over the years. Choosing recovery each day means I must, 'feel the fear and do it anyway.' I must push my boundaries and push past the feeling that I'll be judged and criticised. Past the thoughts that I look fat and ugly. I am writing this blog because I want to learn to be in the moment with those feelings, and then let them go. The feelings of fear and anxiety DO NOT have to stay with me for the remainder of the day, or the week, or even the five minutes.

My self-image is still not amazing. I think this is largely because my body has changed since I gave birth a year ago. There are stretch marks across my stomach, which didn't used to be there, and I'm heavier than perhaps I would like to be. So, of course I'm going to struggle with my eating disordered voice, which tells me I must restrict again to get back down to the size I want to be. Some days I *plan* to restrict a little, some days, I *do* restrict a little. Other days, I can ignore that other voice that lives inside my head, who I call Ethel, although it's hard. That's what recovery is all about, hard *work*. I could have ended my life at fifteen (another blog for another day), but I didn't. I chose to carry on living. I chose to make the next day, and that was a step in recovery. Every choice we make to carry on fighting is a step in recovery.

Some days, I look in the mirror and I feel fantastic. I'm not dressed up; I haven't plastered my face in makeup (I am NOT a makeup person) but I look at myself and I feel confident. I am a mother. I am a friend. I am a daughter. I am a sister. I am a twenty-six-year-old woman with dreams and ambitions. I have had a difficult year, a difficult twelve years! But I'm here. I can look in the mirror and be proud of myself, and feel fantastic, because I'm alive. Because, to some extent, I am free. I'm not one hundred per cent free, I never will be, but I've learnt that I am NOT my mental illnesses. For so many years, I believed truly that I WAS my eating disorder, I WAS my anxiety and there was nothing I could do about it. At fifteen, I believed whole heartedly that I WAS my depression, and life would never improve. I think probably in the last two years,

I've really realised that my mental illnesses do NOT define me. I am my own unique person. I am confident and sarcastic, and I have things I want to do.

So, although looking at myself on videos and vlogs is difficult, and my self-image is not always great, I am still proud of the person I am. I know now, I am NOT my illnesses. My proudest feeling is knowing I am a mother to the most precious child. Knowing that I am my own person, and that I have so many joyful things and people in my life, gives me the love and kindness I need to look in the mirror and say, you are worthy and you are beautiful just as you are. Leonie xox

August 2018 – Blog

So much has happened recently, I don't really know where to begin. So many choices I've made, so many good days and bad. Firstly, what springs to mind, is something GOOD. I have enrolled with the Open University, to study a degree in Religious Studies. I'm hoping afterwards to then do my teacher training and become the teacher I always wanted to be. There have been so many careers I've wanted to experience, but recently I realised something which I think made the decision for me. I realised that I didn't want to be a counsellor until I got my eating disorder and depression at school. From fifteen, I had decided I wanted to be a counsellor and help other young people who had eating disorders. When I had given birth to Alissa, I thought I wanted to become a midwife, because I wanted to help other women go through this massive experience, knowing they weren't alone, and they were supported. Then I got thinking that, all these things

I've wanted to do, are *because* of things that have happened to me... What was before?

Teaching.

It was always teaching. I can't remember a time during primary school when I DIDN'T want to teach. Aside from wanting to be a librarian and use the stamp and ink pad (we ALL wanted to be the librarian that stamps the books, right?) Well, aside from that dream, the only thing I ever wanted to do was teach. The subjects I could never quite decide on, it was always either English, Music, or Religious Studies. I don't really care much about Romeo and Juliet or grade five music theory, but I DO care about faith. Of course, being raised as a Jehovah's Witness, and having such a strong religious family background has played its, but the thing is, religion isn't about right or wrong. Indiana Jones didn't walk out into thin air in film number three to get the cup of Christ and save his Dad because he knew his religion was the right one. He did it because in that moment, he had *faith*. I want to learn and teach about people's different faiths, people's different views of God. The history of all this religion, and how I can use all that knowledge to help young people to understand and appreciate and respect such a variety of religion.

Moving on to a little story about my anxiety. The other day I walked into town and then, I caught a bus. Public transport is a huge deal for me. My anxiety is like a parasite that clings to me from the inside and shoots out fear all around me. To bus by myself was a huge deal and not only did I bus solo, I also, on another day, bussed with Alissa, and they are just small victories which contribute to an overall recovery. Recovery isn't about a big bold statement. You don't walk into rehab and walk out the next day. It's small steps upwards. It's little victories that make you feel like you can do this again. Then you do it again and you realise, after a week, two weeks, a month, that you've been doing it every day, and you don't even give it a second thought anymore. This could be eating with a big spoon, or not separating your food on your plate anymore. It could be getting a bus. That's my small victory. You might be wondering how this possibly helps my recovery with an eating disorder. Well, for me, getting on a bus where people are looking at me, fuels all kinds of ED thoughts. Ethel comes out and starts talking to me as she does, "they're all looking at you" "they can see that your bum is taking up the two seats" "they all know you gained a pound this morning" "why did you get on the bus you're disgusting" Any, sometimes all and more, of these thoughts will suddenly appear, and then I have not just eating disorder anxiety, but general social anxiety too, and it all becomes overwhelming and too much to cope with. Being able to catch the bus and tell Ethel to leave me alone was a win for me. I told her that I gained a pound and it doesn't matter because I'm still getting on that bus. It's me telling my anxiety that I don't need to fear people judging me. I don't need to fear the world, of the small space, of not getting a seat right at the front and having to walk past all these people. Recovery is all about these steps. Steps that make you feel like you're worth something. Worth more than you think. You're a part of this world, and you deserve to be part of this world, and you deserve to be happy in it.

It hasn't all been smooth sailing this week though. I booked a driving lesson in a moment of feeling strong enough, but then the day came, and the anxiety won. I cancelled the lesson and

I haven't rebooked. I have not won this victory, and in my heart, I feel like I won't. Maybe I don't want it enough? I don't know. I don't want to drive but I guess I feel I need to.

I also don't want to feel the burning pain of missing my Dad anymore. I haven't yet shared with you, that whilst I was five months pregnant, my Dad committed suicide. He hanged himself and left devastation for us all. Every day, there's this little bit of me that wakes and thinks of him, and thinks maybe he's still in his little flat, half an hour down the road, and maybe I'll just phone him, and he'll pick up. Of course, I know he's gone, and I know he's not coming back. But I miss him so much that it burns. It physically feels as though there's a little ring of fire burning in my heart, and it slowly keeps getting bigger. Sometimes I just think, I can't believe he's dead. I can't believe he took his own life, when my little life wasn't even in the world yet. The hurt and the pain every day, sometimes I wonder if it'll be too much. I have an anchor to the world now though and that is Alissa. She keeps me here, and I keep strong for her. I sometimes think is it OK that some days the reason I live is because I *have* to for her. I think, it's not really my victory is it, because if I could choose to stay or go, some days, I'd like to go. But I never would, because of her. I don't feel I can be proud of this because this isn't me being strong, it's not me being 'recovered' or 'in recovery', it's me *having* to stay tied to this world, because I **am** tied to this world, because she is here, and she *is* my world. These feelings don't make me suicidal, they just make me human. I am sure at one point or another in all our lives, we have all thought that going to sleep and not waking up would be a much easier alternative than facing something hard the next day.

In other news, my divorce is official and complete. I am no longer a Mrs, but once again a tragic Bridget Jones spinster, only with child. I am no longer someone's wife, but just another singleton, who'll never be the first choice to anyone because I am neither petit nor blonde nor particularly pretty. I am a plain Jane. A boring egg. I am a large broad-shouldered beast, with short curly hair and a nose that is far too big for ones face. My boobs are no longer their perky twenty-year-old selves, but slightly droopier, still big, but not nearly as pretty, twenty-six-year-old breasts. No longer fun boobs, but mature old breasticles, that have fed a child and sit on my stomach like a happy little Buddha. I suppose this takes me onto myself, and my gloomy self-image. I'm tired of looking in the mirror and seeing a tired person looking back. A fat, tired, ogre staring back wondering where it all went wrong. I'm sure at some point in my life I had an actual body shape, now I just seem to be one tubby mess. This blog has been an offload and it's felt good. Leonie xox

August 2018 – Blog

I decided todays blog should be my back story so I'm going to talk about my mental illnesses, and my anxiety first, because it seems to stand alone. Whenever I have a catch up with my Doctor about my anxiety meds or just a general appointment, they always ask how my depression and anxiety are. As though they go together. But they don't, well not for me anyway.

I remember being a child and being happy and confident. I'm not sure when this changed really. Being raised as a Jehovah's Witness meant going on the ministry on Saturday mornings, and as a child, I would do this. I enjoyed doing it, because

I felt independent and confident and like I was making a small difference. Now though, that would terrify me. My anxiety would overcome my whole body, and I wouldn't even make it out in the first place. So how come, at eleven to thirteen, I was able to so freely and confidently knock on door after door and talk about religion and hand out magazines to complete strangers? I think a part of it was that I felt secure because I had this whole group of people surrounding me, and they were all my family. I felt safe and comforted and protected because I was a part of something that made me different, and it was OK. I was proud to be different, and proud to be a Jehovah's Witness. When I left at fourteen, my world changed. I can remember my fourteenth birthday because it was my very first. At school, they did a surprise cake and sang to me and made this big effort. Suddenly though, I didn't feel happy to be sticking out, I felt awkward and embarrassed and I wanted to hide and crawl into a cave and not come out.

I was no longer part of anything special, I was just another kid, another birthday, another ordinary person. Although I liked being able to socialise with friends more and sleep in on Saturday mornings, I felt I'd lost my identity I suppose. I wasn't sure where I fitted in. People knew me as the girl that had to sit out from the assemblies at school, and now suddenly, I wasn't her anymore. I think this is when my anxiety kicked in. My eating disorder and depression also started at this same time, but those two went together, hand in hand. I remember my cousin often inviting me to stay over, and because I was such a people pleaser, I'd say yes. I'd then be overcome with anxiety, worrying that I was far away from home, around people I didn't know, and I had to pretend to be 'cool' just like them. They'd smoke and drink and I'd never done any of this because that wasn't how I was raised. I just didn't belong anywhere. I think from this point on, I've always suffered with anxiety, mostly around places and people I don't know, new situations, and feeling far away from home or safe spaces. At school, as I said, I didn't feel I really belonged to any particular 'group.' I wasn't smart enough to be one of the nerdy kids (nor did I want to be.) I wasn't cool enough to be one of the cool 'emo' kids. I didn't wear makeup, and I certainly didn't have a thin body and long blonde extensions to look like Barbie (unless there's an afro frizzy curly haired beast Barbie I've not yet seen!) I wasn't that smart, I wasn't cool, I wasn't pretty, but I wasn't the worst of the bunch. I wasn't the one you made fun of or tried to play pranks on. I was just somewhere in between. I didn't have a subject that I amazed people with, so I was always left feeling as though I had to constantly fight and work so hard to get good grades. That then somehow turned into me having this idea in my head that I had to get the best grades, and I had to be better than everyone else. *Perfect*.

That word, perfect, it's a funny word. Why do we strive for perfection? Why don't we have the urge to strive for happy, or just bog standard 'OK'? I know, deep down, that perfection doesn't exist, but I strive for it nonetheless, and I still hope that one day I will reach it. At fourteen, I felt the need to become perfect and start getting the highest grades at school because I wasn't special anymore. I needed to be something, someone, so I decided not eating was the best thing to getting me there. By not eating, I would be thinner, healthier, more in control of my life. Then I would be a better person and therefore a brighter person, able to achieve 'perfect' grades.

I started to restrict my calorie intake, which started at eight hundred per day, and slowly went down to three hundred feeling safe, which months down the line, turned into bingeing, which then turned into throwing up, which then turned into a pattern. Which excessive exercise then became a part of. Through this path, I tumbled further and further into someone I didn't know or recognise anymore, and I became just a ghost, a shell, a body. There was nothing in me left to give. I didn't care anymore about grades or school, and yet, I still did deeply. The eating disorder (Ethel) cared for nothing, yet there was still just a small bit of me in there, and she still wanted to be the very best. Ethel stripped me down like I was old mouldy wallpaper waiting to be tossed out. It tore me into pieces and left nothing inside. I became empty and I felt nothing anymore. There wasn't even the great sadness that had been there so many times, on so many days, often after throwing up, whilst holding onto the sides of the sink, where the tears would start to fall. In the end, Ethel took so much, and gave such little back, so depression found me curled up and withered on the floor and it took me whole. I felt like nothing. I was nothing and I had nothing left for people around me. My spark, my light, my soul was gone, and things just became numb.

I'll talk more about what led on from there in another blog, but this is the start, where it began. I am thankful that my illnesses found me, because I wouldn't be *me* without them. From all this great sadness, I found great hope and great light. When I emerged into my first recovery period, I shone. I was so happy, so healthy and so full of *life* again. I was seventeen when I felt like I had beaten it. I didn't know then of course, that it was a monster that would always remain tucked away inside me, but for that time, in college, I was *free*. My mental illnesses led me to my future, and that college course, which I wouldn't have chosen if not for my eating disorder, found me a best friend who remains today, ten years on. Our mental illnesses take us and destroy us, but they also give us a direction in life we would not take if not for them. It's been twelve years since I first got my eating disorder, anxiety and depression and yet, here I am. I'm still here, and even though I'm still sick, and will never be one hundred per cent 'OK', it doesn't matter. I'm still here. If that isn't a small victory, a small step of recovery, I don't know what is. Leonie xox

August 2018 – Blog

Today my ex-husband picked up my baby girl, as he does on a Sunday, but last week, he just turned up with his new girlfriend (bearing in mind we've been divorced a month),and then lied about their plans for the day. I of course had a full-on anxiety attack, with hyperventilating and palpitations and I cried endlessly because I wanted my baby home. Being a Mum has given me a new level of anxiety with just the thought of Alissa going with other people, triggering off a panic in me.

I'm trying very hard, to embark on a new self-love journey. Lately, I've been feeling like the problem with a lot of us, is that we don't love ourselves. We love others unconditionally, yet, we don't give the same love to ourselves. So, I'm adamant that I *can*, and I *will* show myself the love I deserve. I may not like certain bits of myself. I may not enjoy the fact my stomach now looks like a tiger's body, and that, in my mind, I'm so tall and wide I look like Shrek (minus the green), but I can try to love myself. I can love that I have given birth to the most beautiful human being on this planet (subjective of course), and that the scar on my right knee came from a truly fun day with my big sister when I was younger. I can love that my curly hair comes from my Caribbean roots, and I can love that I have a creative personality and enjoy anything arty and book wormy and a little bit geeky.

I think self-love is so important, and I'm disappointed that I haven't been loving myself all these years. I watched a film last night, I can't remember the title, but it was about a black woman who had afro hair. She had been raised to believe that her hair was ugly and unattractive, and not perfect. It was drummed into her that she had to have straightened perfect hair to be the perfect version of herself. She feared rain and humidity because of what it did to her hair (which I can relate to with my traumatic straightening disasters during my school days).

Throughout the film, which is based on her hair, she has it straightened and long, then cuts it short and sleek and dyes it blonde. Then she has a meltdown and shaves it off. After she accepts what she's done, she starts to realise that her hair does NOT make her perfect and she starts on a journey of self-love. She starts to even *like* and enjoy her hair and at the end of the film, it's short, it's afro, and it's HER.

Self-love is about realising who you are, realising that how you were born IS your perfect. Although I say there's no such thing as perfection (even though during relapse I constantly try and find it), your natural self, IS your perfect self. If you're born with frizzy locks, embrace them. If you're born with ginger hair and strawberry freckles, own it. Whoever you are, at the *core*, is exactly who you're meant to be. Leonie xox

August 2018 – Blog

I want to talk to people who were a part of my past, at the start of where my mental illness all began, in order to release some feelings but I'm wondering if I'm ready. I don't want to hear that I've hurt the people I love from my past actions. I'm scared to hear it, I'm scared to bring it up, and I'm scared to relive it. I don't want to hear about the time I tried to kill myself, and my Mum had to come home to the police. I don't want to hear about my Mum questioning my laxative abuse after finding them in my knicker drawer (funnily enough, I had never actually taken them during that time, and bought that pack as an emergency. Not sure my Mum ever believed me though.) That's a good reason why I would like to talk to people, to clear the air, to confess the things I lied about, and the things they *think* I lied about. But I'm scared to, and now, I don't want to. I flip between wanting to be proactive in my recovery and make these giant steps, to becoming scared all over again, staying in my secure bubble. Some days I can be on top of the world, but others, I just crave curling up in bed and sleeping forever. Today is one of those days. I don't feel depressed, or even anxious, and my eating disorder is not presently whispering in my ear. I just feel flat. Not even bored. Just flat. I can't really explain the feeling properly. I just don't feel much at all today. I'm missing Alissa and no matter how much I crave my weekends now, as soon as she's away from me, I instantly want her home. I miss her giggle, the way she runs and looks like a little drunk elf. I miss her random babbling and the way she says 'wa' for water. I miss that when she doesn't want to do something, she now says 'no' in the funniest way. I miss my baby. Leonie xox

August 2018 – Blog

I feel incredibly emotional, but I had a realisation last week I wanted to share. I was lying in bed and suddenly a thought came into my head out of nowhere and it was this. I don't want my eating disorder back. It was *such* a revelation! I can't honestly tell you how shocked I was to realise it and think it. I thought I always wanted Ethel back in full blast, because it would get me to where I wanted to be, and it'd give me back the control I need to succeed in life. The thing is though, now that I'm a mother, my whole outlook on life has changed so much. I really don't want my eating disorder back, ever.

I don't want any part of that twisted illness back in my life. This is such a massive thing for me to finally realise and it makes me so happy! Although I still have little habits from my eating disorder that I think I'll always have, and although I may go through periods where I count my calories and freak out over my food consumption and weight, mentally, I am in a really good place at the moment. I just wanted to share this with you all because it just came as such a surprise and I am so glad the thought just popped into my head. It's just helped me see how much I've changed and grown as a person and how well I'm doing. I might be a divorced spinster, single mother and have no job and no life other than nappies and poo… Lots of poo. I don't want to be sick like I was ever again though and that's great. Leonie xox

August 2018 – Blog

I've had no sleep at all. Alissa is teething badly and she's up most of the night. She walks to my bed at some point, last night was ten o'clock, and gets into my bed for the rest of the night. It's lovely to have her close by and I've never had a problem with co-sleeping, but she either wants to have her face on my face because she 'isn't close enough', or she is kicking me and lying the length of the pillow instead of the length of the bed. I've noticed how my lack of sleep makes everything so much harder in my recovery. I find everything harder and I feel awful, I look awful, and I just don't even want to try at recovery. I don't even want to make the small steps towards happiness and health. Last night I had some strong Ethel thoughts and I really wanted to take some laxatives. I don't know why that thought appeared though, but I feel that the tiredness really messes with my mental health. Working at recovery is a lot harder when I'm sleep deprived. I know it's not meant to be easy; I know it's hard work to fight for your good mental health, but some days I just don't want to. Leonie xox

August 2018 – Blog

This morning I had a thought that popped into my head. I was doing some colouring and I went out the lines for the first time after being nudged by my little monster of a child who I love enormously. Immediately, I thought, great, it's ruined. There's no point carrying on because I've ruined it. It's not perfect anymore. Then I stopped, and this thought just came to me. Why does it matter? Who cares if I went out the lines. Me. Why do I care? Does it look any less beautiful, *no*. I carried on even though there was a part of me that didn't want to, and I coloured every little bit in and I look at it now and... It's beautiful. It's *not* perfect. It's nowhere even close. But it's colourful and it shines. It has meaning to it and each part tells a story, each colour I chose, each area I coloured. It's perfectly IMPERFECT.

Perfection, for me, is a massive thing. I'm worried about February. My course starts and I know my need for perfection, my need to be the very best will kick in. I know I'll want to get the very best results, and I know I'll do whatever it takes to get there. This might mean relapse. It scares me, sure. But also, it reminds me. Reminds me that this disease is always here, and it takes hard work to beat it. Recovery is about working hard. I could have given up today, I could have let this beautiful colouring go in the bin. But instead, it's on my fridge, reminding me that the sun has risen. I do see it, I feel it, and I see a whole world around me, and it's beautiful. Mental illness strips us from seeing the beauty in the world. It takes away our eyesight and it just leaves a foggy grey black mist where we are blinded. I refuse to be blind anymore. It's time to see again. Some days are more painful, some days are harder and some days I want to stop colouring in and give up, because I've gone outside the lines and ruined my recovery. Do I? No way. Why? Because at the end, I know, and I must believe, that the final picture will be truly beautiful in its own imperfections. Today, I believe. Leonie xox

August 2018 – Blog

I had to answer this question whilst it's on my mind. Someone asked me how I'm coping with my breakup and if it's contributing to my recovery in a bad way. Whilst I tell myself I don't love my ex-husband anymore, and I'm happy that he's moved on so quickly, I suppose there must be something still there, because I feel bitter, and sad and resentful and all the other negative emotions you feel. I'm not happy that he's moved on. Not because I want him, but because I'm so angry that he didn't love me enough when we were together. I'm angry that I was his 'tester' relationship. I was just the first thing that came along after his previous breakup and he used me. I'm still so angry, and so hurt.

I'm not in love with him anymore, and I don't even think I love any part of him. I'm just sad that whilst I gave him my whole heart, he cheated, lied and betrayed me. He made me feel worthless and as though I was nothing. He squashed me, little by little, every day, until one day I had no spark left. I started to believe that I had no talents, no skills, that I couldn't do anything. He'd laugh at me, and jokingly tell me I was useless.

It is hard having to still see him (he comes to see Alissa twice a week in the evenings and has her once at the weekend), but my mental health is better without him in my life. There are little fleeting moments where I look at his new girlfriend and wonder if it was because I was too fat, had too many stretch marks, had frizzy hair and didn't bother with makeup. I wonder if I had looked like a model, if he'd have loved me more.

Of course, this then makes me want to starve, take laxatives, punch my stomach, and all the other horrible things we do to ourselves. But I won't let my eating disordered thoughts win. Without him, I've learnt that I'm OK. I've learnt that I am capable of so much more than he ever led me to believe. I've learnt that I have passion, and with it, power. This breakup truly broke my heart at first. But he broke it more. Crying for him has no way been nearly as bad as my crying when I was *with* him. I literally would hug my heart with my hands, because it felt like it was physically breaking. He'd shout at me when we argued, and I him, but I loved him so much that he was still so wonderful in my eyes. Over time, he broke my soul, my spirit and my '*self*'. The worth, the care, the love. All the 'self.'

The breakup has contributed to my recovery in a good way. Though there are some days I still hurt, most days I lift my head up, and I smile because I made it. I took a leap of faith, that being by myself with my daughter would be better than being in a relationship that had become toxic. I was right. The day I left him, I made another step towards my recovery. Now, the things I was once told I couldn't do, I do daily. The passion he took from me, I've got back. The voice that told me I wasn't good enough is going. I am brave, bruised, and I am *me*. Leonie xox

September 2018 – Blog

Yesterday I was tearful because I was meeting a mum friend for coffee and I looked awful. I get anxious anyway, because it's a bus journey away and I was worrying about bussing with Alissa so my wonderful Mum took Alissa for me so I didn't have to worry about getting back with her and she also gave me a lift there which was great. I then walked home. The point I wanted to make, was that my friend didn't care. She didn't even mention it. I was tearful, anxious and felt like the ugliest most disgusting human on the Earth, but it didn't matter to her. She was happy to see me, and I was happy to see her. I cuddled her beautiful six-month-old bubba and we had a moan about life and a laugh about our babies.

She just made me realise something. I might feel hideous. I might look in the mirror and feel fat, ugly, spotty, like scales are covering my body. But my TRUE friends, my family, my ones who love me unconditionally. They don't care. It doesn't matter what I look like to them because they love me for who I am, on the inside. I started the day not wanting to leave the house, for fear of people looking at me and wondering why I looked like a monster. I had to force myself to go out. I didn't even want my Mum to see me. I wanted to hide away from the world and cease to exist yesterday. But I didn't. I went out, I saw my friend, and I had a really good time. I pushed myself yesterday, and because of it, I feel I've had a little victory. I feel today, I hold my head a little higher and smile a little wider. The people that love me, love ME. Not what I look like or what I'm wearing. Just me. That is another small step of recovery. Leonie xox

September 2018 – Blog

I read this today; "*As someone with low self-confidence, you tend not to feel comfortable interacting with other people. Although you find the company of friends pleasant, you tend to feel uneasy meeting new people and interacting with strangers. Your discomfort socialising sometimes makes it difficult for you to make new friends. Perhaps because you do not particularly like talking about yourself, others find it difficult to develop an accurate impression of who you are. This weak social confidence likely stems from your personal beliefs about yourself. Although you have several strengths, you tend be somewhat critical of yourself and have difficulty overcoming your perceived weaknesses. For example, you tend to regret things that you've done or said in the past and* get embarrassed somewhat easily. When it comes to your professional life, you tend to set low to moderate standards for yourself. These unrealistically low standards may perpetuate your tendency to think that you're less competent than you truly are. Chances are, you find the advice and support of friends more compelling than your own advice. As someone who is oriented to familial matters, you value the company of family-members and domestic life. If you have children already, you enjoy spending time with them very much and work hard to be a good parent. If you don't have children, you very much desire having children in the future. What really sets you apart from people that are low in family orientation is that you know how to manage your frustrations and work well on your own. This means that you are well-equipped to manage a family without letting all the work that is involved wear you down. However, as someone with strong family values, all the work that is involved in maintaining a tidy home and well-stocked kitchen might occasionally make it difficult for you to finish everything that you need to do. As someone high in openness, you have a strong appreciation for beauty, both in art and nature. Indeed, it's likely that you are easily absorbed in music and art, as well as natural phenomena. Another aspect of your openness is your emotional insight; that is, you probably have good access to and awareness of your own emotions. Another aspect of the openness dimension is the tendency to think about abstract concepts and ideas. This thinking style may take the form of artistic and metaphorical use of language, and/or music composition or performance. Thus, it is likely that, either in your work or spare time, you enjoy activities that get your "creative juices" flowing."

This is so accurate and it's a little scary that a computer can analyse me from some questions and get my personality so spot on. It's given me something to think about and reflect on though and that's good for my recovery, I think. Leonie xox

September 2018 – Blog

Sometimes I think that I must be OK, and not suffer from anxiety, because day to day for the most part I am OK. Something happened today that reminded me that no, I'm *not* OK, and I *do* still suffer from very bad anxiety. My ex mother in law has Alissa most Saturdays for the afternoon and she usually brings her home around five-thirty. Today, at five o'clock, I text her to say let me know when you're leaving, and I'll come out when you arrive as it's cold out and I'll bring a blanket to wrap Alissa up in. She agreed and I didn't then text again. Six o'clock came and went, which is her bedtime, and my anxiety went completely through the roof. I started imagining all the worst things. I text her asking if everything was OK and received no reply (she was driving and had forgotten to text to tell me she was leaving). I had to busy myself because the thoughts that were coming into my head about my baby not being OK were too much to handle. I started washing up, then went into the bathroom and started scrubbing and cleaning whilst hyperventilating. I felt as though my chest was going to burst with the panic. My breathing was ridiculously heavy and my eyes stinging with tears that I was trying to hold back. She text me to tell me they were outside, and it took everything I had not to break apart at that moment with relief and fear and love and every emotion a human can feel. I never want to let my baby out my sight again. Anxiety is so silly but, in the moment, it's so real and raw and so hard to control and think rationally about. So often, I think that I'm OK, that I must be OK, because to the world I *look* OK. But just because we look OK on the outside, doesn't mean we're not truly breaking apart on the inside. Leonie xox

October 2018 – Blog

Yesterday, I received a letter telling me that a benefit I receive is due to end on Christmas Eve. Immediately, I went into anxiety attack mode again. I phoned them and was told I needed to phone a different benefit line because they were now taking this benefit over (if you don't know the benefit system, I pray you never have to!) I spent thirty minutes (no exaggerating), waiting for the first phone call to be picked up. I then spent another twenty minutes waiting for the second benefit person to answer my call. I had a very lovely and helpful man speak to me, and he really did his best to explain. The situation seems to be, if I don't pass some medical assessment that justifies that I'm mentally ill, then from December twenty-fifth, I won't receive any extra money. Well, of course, I then started to have a proper panic attack on the phone, trying not to cry, whilst my heartbeat could be heard by the elephants in Africa!

I'm really scared of this medical assessment, because on the face of it, I look and seem happy. I'm always together, presentable, I don't have trouble washing and getting dressed because of my mental state and I don't need additional support to find a job. My problems are those that cannot be seen clearly. They have roots that go so far below the surface, they're almost unreachable. I don't even know why I quit job after job sometimes. Why my fear of being tired at work is so intense. Why I had to have an anxiety attack in a cupboard at one job and then tell them I felt sick so I could go home and email to quit, after just one day of work. I don't know why the thought of getting on a bus with a pushchair makes me feel physically sick. I can explain these things to them, sure, but they're not going to see me having a panic attack whilst I have this assessment. So now, I sit here typing to you, almost crying (again), because I am so scared that they're going to think I'm perfectly fine and perfectly normal. If that happens, I'll lose three hundred pounds a month which pays my bills and my food for Alissa for the month. I can't lose that money. I can't get a job with Alissa, I won't hold down a job because of my anxiety, and I am freaking out so much. Unexpected chaos makes recovery so much harder because I just want to relapse hard and get sick, so they see that I'm not OK and that I *am* ill. I don't know what to do anymore. Leonie xox

October 2018 – Blog

On Thursday Alissa first showed signs of hand foot and mouth. She woke up perky as usual, and the minor grizzles she had, I put down to teething. She was due to be looked after by my Mum from ten-thirty Thursday morning, as I was meeting a friend who lives about forty-five minutes away and about half an hour on a bus to a slightly closer town that was convenient for us both to meet. My Mum got her, and I got on the bus... I had only just arrived in town when I got a call from my Mum saying Alissa really wasn't well and was burning hot and she thought I should come home right away. So, for anyone with anxiety or other mental illnesses, this was my WORST NIGHTMARE. I already got on the bus by myself, which is a *huge* step for me, one which I've spoken about before. I hate being stuck on the bus, knowing I'm surrounded by people who are looking at me and thinking all sorts of horrible things about me; fat, ugly, whale, beast etc. Nightmare one. But I owned those feelings on Thursday and got on the bus because you know what, I wasn't going to let mental illness take me that day. I needed a good coffee with my friend and a good chat. Suddenly though, I was stuck in this town half an hour away from home and I can *hear* my baby crying on the phone and there's nothing I can do about it. If you're a parent, then you'll know how this feels but anyone can relate to this. Someone you love is screaming down the phone and calling for you and you're far away, with no way to get to them quickly. Nightmare two. My anxiety had never been so high. As it happened, for added drama (I promise you I'm not making any of this up), my friends phone had no signal so I couldn't reach her. I had to go to the bus stop without even saying hello or telling her I'd arrived and now I was going again. Luckily, as I got to the bus stop her phone connected and she ran to me to hear the story before I left. I sat on the bus crying, anxious, hyperventilating, and feeling as though my mental illnesses are right.

The voices in my head won that day. My anxiety tells me the worst possible things are going to happen if I go out into the world and mix with society. They did. Hearing my baby calling 'Mumma' and screaming as her temperature raised over forty degrees, and not being able to cuddle her, literally clawed my heart out. I sat on the bus knowing it couldn't go any faster but willing it to and praying that there'd be no one waiting at each stop. I then realised I had given my Mum my keys because she might need to get into my flat. My Mum was half an hour away in the other direction, attending a hospital appointment for my little sister ironically (so the nurses there took Alissa's temperature.) Anxiety then kicked in again at the thought of waiting outside my front door where people would probably pass and wonder what I was doing, have a good look at me, looking a state, and not be able to fit past me because I'm so massive. Anxiety... Please... For all our sakes. GO AWAY!!

Thursday showed me that a lot of the time our anxiety is a huge exaggeration of what could happen, and most of the time what we *think* is going to happen, doesn't. But, it could also happen just the way you fear it and so I will probably not get on a bus for a very long time. My anxiety over being far away from home has increased A LOT and more importantly, Thursday was a reminder for me that recovery is ongoing, hard work. I started the day with a little victory towards my recovery. I tackled my anxiety voice and pushed it aside and got on that bus and went away from my home, my safe place. I ended the day anxious and distraught... But I did give it a go. Leonie xox

October 2018 – Blog

I wanted to talk about my experience with laxatives. I remember once, at sixteen I think, I asked my Mum to buy me some bananas as she was heading to the shop, ironically just before heading to the loo for a wee. I remember her tone of voice and her reply and everything about that moment. I don't remember the exact words, but they were along the lines of "not if you're just going to get rid of them with laxatives." I felt so embarrassed at that moment, and more than that, I suppose I felt found out. I felt exposed that she'd found my laxatives, hidden away in my bra and pants drawer. (SIDE

NOTE: Who else combines their bras and pants in the one drawer, then has a whole other drawer just for socks, when in fact, you have about five pairs of socks but fifty bras and hundreds of pants? Anyone?) The hilarious, and very truthful thing is, I'd *never* taken laxative pills before in my life, and I didn't take any of those that she found. I didn't discover laxative pills until 2015, during the lead up to my wedding. Before this, I had done laxatives exactly one time and one time only. During school, a few swigs of a disgusting syrup which led to a nice happy surprise when I stepped on the scale the next morning and was four pounds lighter. You'd think because I had such good results that I would have kept this up and continued, but when I was fifteen, my control came from simply not eating. I did binge and I did make myself sick, but that was, (and this is coming from fifteen-year-old me), 'for fun'.

Back to laxatives for now. In 2015, at the beginning of the year, I'd just got engaged and I had until August, the month of my wedding. So, I'm losing weight and I've relapsed. From January through to the end of the year, I relapsed badly. I had gained back my 'control' that I'd lost for a while (because I was HEALTHY you stupid eating disordered Ethel, get back in your cave.) One day, I was at work, working as a receptionist at a doctor's surgery, and I felt awful. I was bloated I guess, I'm not sure what it was, but my stomach just felt hard as a rock and painful to touch. I thought I looked severely pregnant. I got home after work and I don't know where it came from, but a sudden thought appeared. 'Laxatives will solve this, why haven't I thought of this before.' That was that really. I took them once, my rock-hard painful stomach went away, and an empty 'clean' feeling came with it. From then on, I thought it'd be OK to just take a few every now and again. You're supposed to take up to two, but as time went on, the number grew and grew and within one month I was hooked on them. It happened that quickly and they took control of my life faster than a fart. I was taking more and more to get the same effect, and because I wasn't eating anything aside from a few crackers a day, I ended up literally just getting rid of water. Funnily enough, this is how I liked it, because it meant I was 'pure'. I was the cleanest I could be because there was *nothing* inside me. I was rid of everything. When that feeling came, I felt high. I felt amazing. I had learnt how to take them so that they worked in the early hours of the morning and then by the time I had to get up for work, they'd finished, and I could go about my normal day. I had it all under control, and luckily (believe me, I was LUCKY), I never had any embarrassing accidents.

As the months passed, the wedding approached, and I just needed to feel nothing. My relationship wasn't happy, even then, and at one point I suggested we call it all off, but my ex-husband wouldn't hear of it. I think he was embarrassed about telling everyone we weren't going to get married after all. The wedding remained booked and I remained hooked on laxatives. I tried a few times to stop taking them, and maybe managed a day, two at most. It had become so easy to just swallow these pills with a sip of water. So easy to take and forget about and then remember when the stomach cramps would wake me at three in the morning. Eventually, I ended up in outpatient treatment at an eating disorder clinic, and the clinician there told me I had very low electrolytes and my laxative addiction had become dangerous. I suppose that put the first niggle in my head that I should perhaps stop for good. The second was when I collapsed at work and they called the paramedics out to me. I hadn't eaten anything, I was tired, cold, dead inside. I was drunk on laxative addiction and I was properly ill this time. I knew it. They knew it. It was time to change. I'm not sure what happened then, I can't remember when the day came where I just didn't take them anymore. I just didn't. I remember wanting to take them the night before my wedding, but I couldn't because I wasn't at home and I obviously didn't want to risk it on my wedding day. It makes me sad to think that instead of being giddy about my wedding, I was annoyed, worried and felt as though I'd lost control because I couldn't take laxatives and I knew I'd have to eat the day of my wedding.

When I did stop, I think for a few days, maybe four or five, I didn't 'go', and I was worried my body would never be able to work properly without them. (SIDE NOTE: hilarious how I'm now being all British and shy writing 'go' when all I've talked about is poo for the last ten minutes.) There are days now, when the urge to buy laxatives is strong. The addiction I had to them was powerful and it meant something to me. It meant I had life under control. It meant that although my relationship was falling apart, and my life was sad, I could still be better. Do better. Win. At what I don't know.

On the days when I think about buying a sneaky pack to keep 'just in case', I stop and look at them and look at them hard. I remember what they did to me mentally and how those pills lined up every night on my bedside cabinet, wasn't healthy. I remember that I am more than that and I am stronger than that. Although difficult, I do it every time. Perhaps because I have Alissa. Perhaps because I'm a mother and I'm needed in the world. Perhaps because I'm stronger now, I don't know. But I do it. That's a small step towards recovery that I'm proud of. Leonie xox

October 2018 – Blog

Let's talk about self-harm and suicide. In at least three sessions with different CBT therapists, counsellors, clinicians etc, I've been labelled as suicidal because I've spoken about self-harm... No thank you. Take that post it note off my shoulder and put it back on your very expensive notebook. Not right, not true and not accurate. I want to talk about my experience with them separately, and together, so let's start with self-harm. I can't remember the first time I self-harmed. I was fifteen, and I was extremely low but I don't remember where the trigger came from or what I was doing. I can't remember if I was at home or at school, and I can't remember what I used. So, I will tell you about the overall experience instead. I never enjoyed the feeling of a deep, bloody cut. I never enjoyed trying to get to the bone, and it was never about that for me. My self-harm was all about small slices, quick and efficient, releasing a feeling that I didn't want to acknowledge. I would do these little slices all up and down my legs and arms, and they'd sting and burn, and I loved the feeling. Much like the laxatives, it was truly addictive behaviour. My world then was all about being perfect. My big sister was the rebel and I was the good girl. I didn't drink, I didn't smoke, I didn't have sex, I didn't *do* anything, except get good grades. To keep this up, or to keep this appearance up should I say, I needed a release. Inside, I was screaming. But on the outside, I was composed and together, calm and collected. I'd pick up a pair of scissors usually, and I'd just do these quick little releases of pain, that reminded me I was *real*. They reminded me the pain I felt inside I could lose for just two seconds, as I felt a strong pain on the outside. There were always two parts to my self-harm. The first was from a deep depression. A hatred of my body and my soul that made me want to die inside. This feeling of pure pain was so strong, and I wanted to just disappear into a blackness and never emerge. I had to get this out, I couldn't keep it on my heart. It was heavy and brutal, and it was chained to me like an anchor, dragging me further into a blackness that I could never escape. This first part *did* go hand in hand with suicide, because I just wanted to die. The second part to self-harm was not related to suicide though. There were times, many times, when it became a happiness for me. Cutting just for the thrill of it; that quick sharp feeling was addictive and enjoyable.

Suicide is such a different feeling though and only twice have I been close to ending my life. There have been many wants, plans, feelings of, and wishes. But just two moments, where suicide was an almost reality and I don't remember the events properly. The first I'll keep short and sour because I don't want to reflect on it. It was a dark time in my life, and I don't need to go back there, I'm past it and it was a different time. A different me. My friend and I planned all day and I felt the surest I've ever felt in my entire life. There was no doubt in my mind, no tiny fraction of me that didn't want to go through with it. My best friend wasn't quite ready though so because of her, really, I guess the events that followed meant that we lived another day to tell the tale and I phoned someone close to my heart to say goodbye and obviously didn't think at the time, being fifteen, that would mean the police would have to be called out and drama would ensue.

That was the first time that I've ever been less than five minutes away from ending my life. The other time, came later, in adulthood, during my marriage, where arguments were frequent, and the pain was too much to bear again. I took some pills and regretted it, and the pills I took wouldn't have done anything major, it was just a cry for help.

When my Dad killed himself, and I felt the raw pain of losing someone I loved so much, I realised I would *never* do that to my family. Never. I could never hurt them that way and leave that pain behind for Alissa to grow with. Thankfully, I never feel that deep depression anymore. That's gone, and I'm not sure when it went but it's gone for good. I love life for the most part, and more importantly, most days, I love me.

Suicide and self-harm do not go together like wine and cheese (I've never tried wine and cheese, but I hear they're a delicious combination). Like I said, there was a part of me at times that loved to self-harm. It made me happy, it made me feel great and it didn't come from a place of needing to because I was depressed. It came from a place of *wanting* to. I can see now, however, that the reason I self-harmed either way, happy or depressed, was because I needed to *feel,* and I didn't know how to express emotion.

When you can't get out that feeling inside, or you talk to people but don't feel like they're really hearing you, that is when you feel the need to do something *to* you. It might be starving yourself; it might be eating a whole cheesecake with a fork sat on the floor crying (yes, I have been there), it might be popping pills, or it might be self-harming. What we need to learn to do today is more talking about our feelings, and less taking it upon ourselves to feel something other than what's really going on inside.

I feel so fortunate that suicidal fifteen-year-old me got to live. She lived and she grew, and she changed, and she saw the world and experienced its beauty. I am here, I am alive. I am strong and powerful, and I am surviving. My reflection is my recovery for the day and I'm proud of what I've achieved. Leonie xox

October 2018 – Blog

Today at dinner time, I had to stop, think and change. I was feeding my baby rice and pasta and she was very happily eating this, along with her peas and fish, and as she picked up a bit of clumped together rice and pasta (which made me gag), I jokingly said "is that stodgy dinner nice, yum yum." Now obviously I said this because she is fifteen months old and doesn't understand the sentence. She heard the yum yum and happily carried on eating her dinner. But I had to stop, take a moment and realise that this is one of my biggest fears. I am *petrified* that I am going to pass on my disordered thoughts and feelings to her. I am so scared that she's going to grow up thinking it's not normal to use a big spoon because I can't bear to use a big spoon. I'm so scared that she's going to see me rip the middle bit of bread out of the roll because it is too doughy. I'm scared that she's going to look at me and think that what I do is OK, when it's not. I watch comments being said around my nine-year-old sister, and I know she takes them on board. Little things, that to someone who's never had any issues with food wouldn't give a second thought about.

It's too easy today to influence our young cubs, to make them believe that they should be something they're not, look a certain way and eat this and not eat that. My worst fear – I'm the biggest influence of all in my child's life. I called my child's dinner stodgy and disgusting because I'm petrified of stodgy foods. They genuinely scare me, and especially 'white' versions of them, which my baby must have due to allergies. Feeding her is difficult for me, some days I'll admit I really do struggle. But I do it because the love I have for her is greater than anything I'll ever know. I don't want to make any mistakes, but I especially don't want my fears around food, to become *her* fears around food.

Today made me realise just how easy it is to make comments that could damage and niggle away at tiny minds. More importantly, it made me realise just how big a fear this is for me and how I need to work hard to make sure that my thoughts and feelings around Alissa's food aren't shared unless they're positive. I don't *ever* want my baby to worry about food, weight, numbers, body image etc, to an excessive degree, and I certainly don't want to ever be the reason she does. Today reminded me that whilst I would say I'm at the strong end of recovery currently, it's always there. All of it. The eating disorder, the anxiety. While a mentally healthy person may worry for two minutes and then let this thought go, an anxious me takes it to a whole new level of panicking. While most would think nothing of the comment because she's a baby, anxious eating disordered Ethel is shouting at me from the inside out. Why does mental illness take so much from us, *all the time*? Why is it a constant battle and why are they always there, waiting for a good opportunity. Oh, you stepped in a puddle today and made your jeans wet... Well

HERE I AM, Arthur the Anxiety at your service. Everyone will be looking at you now, you can't go into places looking like that. What are you going to do? You can't go home, you're too far away... Arthur, please, just go away. I don't even have the energy to shout at you. Just dive yourself back down into whatever hole you came from and stay there until I really need you, in a situation that I should genuinely be anxious about. I'm sick and tired of letting mental illness creep in every second of the day, unnecessarily.

My goal for this weekend – every time an anxious thought comes near, put it into perspective. Is it necessary? Probably not. Is it going to kill me or hurt someone? Probably not. Then DO ONE mental illness. I want all my mental illnesses to take a long, overdue holiday and never come back. Leonie xox

October 2018 – Blog

I want to talk about triggers today. I think it's so important that we know our triggers, know what makes us slip into that feeling of depression, anxiety, or the feeling that makes us want to starve, binge and purge. We need to be aware of them, but more importantly we need to *not* fear them. When I was fifteen, I thought my trigger was my parents not being together. They'd been divorced since I was around five, so this wasn't a new thing but somehow, I brought the feeling of hurt from their divorce with me all those years and I was adamant that if they were still together and we were a happy family, I'd be OK. I'd be 'normal.' I quickly learnt that this wasn't the reason I got sick. It may have played a small part in why I felt lost and alone. I may have looked at the other girls in my class who had seemingly 'perfect' lives because their parents were still together. I may have felt jealousy and envy... No, I *did* feel jealousy and envy. I wanted to be part of a normal family. I wanted for once, to just walk in the door to a Mum and a Dad who loved me and cared for me. But that wasn't my trigger, it wasn't even close. My trigger, which I've spoken about before, is the need to be perfect, in control, and achieve the very best. Always has been, always will be. Even in primary school, I can remember getting excellent school reports, so the next school report had to be better. I can remember my teacher telling me how good I was, and what a role model to the other children I was. I can remember getting the biggest ticks in my workbooks and always working hard. I remember once, we had to make a pair of slippers and I used one slipper to do the stencil for the other, but I didn't flip it over, so I ended up with two right feet. The sheer embarrassment when I'd finished making my slippers and realising what I'd done was probably the first time I felt anxiety, although I didn't know it at the time. Getting the best grades was something I was good at. In a world where I didn't feel I ever shone, I could shine through my work. The thing is though, I have never been very talented. I can do things like paint, draw, write etc, but none of them are a real gift. I'm not amazing at the piano, I just worked through my grade books to get to where I am now. I can't just sit and whack out Mozart, I learn the music, repeatedly, note by note, until I know it. My point is, I work hard for the best grades. It's never been a natural gift for me. I watched my big sister just fly through her exams, barely revising, whilst I had to study hour after hour, just to get an average mark. When I started getting my first As and A*s in coursework, I then felt I had to keep it up, so I just kept working harder, until finally, it was too much. The weight on my shoulders became too much, so I needed to become lighter.

That was my first ever trigger for my eating disorder and the biggest one I'll ever have but I also have small triggers, that pop up every now and again, as voices in my head. My anxiety triggers are here all the time, and they drive me insane. I need to go to the shop, which is just five minutes away, but these little triggers start filling my head, and it can take hours for me to muster the strength to leave the house. Little voices saying, 'what if.' What if Alissa starts screaming and people look at me thinking I'm a bad Mum. What if it rains, I don't have a coat on; what if everyone can see my thighs jiggle as I walk. And so, it goes on, what if this, what if that. Similarly, my little eating disordered voice is there also, sending little triggers constantly. You look fat in that, you're ugly in this. If you go out, you'll buy this to eat because you have no self-control. The voices are there all the time, and are a constant, heavy strain. They tire me out, and wear me down, and some days, I really don't believe I can succeed at this recovery nonsense. The thing is though, I should remember that I'm strong enough now to recognise these little triggers. They're alarm bells that go off in my brain, alerting me that I need to pause, remind myself that I am enough, remind myself to ignore the voices, and carry on with my day. It's difficult sometimes, but I truly believe if we *know* our triggers, if we understand what makes our brains tick, then we have the power to also stand still, take a moment, and tell them to leave us alone.

It all starts with the mind, right? So *know* your mind. Understand how it works, and then use your strength and your power to be the person you want to be, without the illness. My little trigger went off today because I had a bath for the first time in a week (that's right, a week, you heard me and yes, I do smell), and during the undressing period, my voices were there telling me all kinds of mean things. My trigger came to the surface and told me that I'd be better if I was smaller, thinner, and if I got back the control I'd lost. For a moment, guilt set in that I had a slice of toast with avocado for lunch, and guilt set in that I'd eaten some chocolate, and guilt set in that I even had the *nerve* to go into the food cupboard... But hold on a minute, wait one second. Who are *you* to tell me I don't deserve to eat food from my own kitchen? You're a mean bully (no, not you, you're just a fabulous reader – I'm clearly talking to my eating disorder, keep up).

Know the trigger, understand it, and use your strength to get rid of it. Even if it's just for a second. So, you, yes eating disorder, Ethel, you mean girl, get back in your hole so I can have a nice bath without worrying what I look like. Today, my baby waddled on in, looked at me and said "boobies", and "belly", and then gave me a kiss. She loves me for all I am, and she certainly doesn't care about my jiggly bits, so why should I? Leonie xox

November 2018 – Blog

This morning I was looking for a hat to wear because it's freezing outside, when I came across my Dad's hat. I can't explain what happened next really. I can't put into the words the meltdown I had. It still smells of him, of his smell. I had to physically clutch at my heart to stop it from breaking out of my chest and cry silent tears, so my beautiful baby didn't wonder what was wrong with her Mummy. I thought grief was meant to be done. It's been nearly two years since he died. Wow. Two years in February. It just feels like yesterday he left us. Left me. I thought that the pain of losing him was meant to have gone now, surely, I can't keep going through life thinking of him and instantly crying? I can't find things of his and have a breakdown in five years? Can I? They say there's no time limit to grief. Well, can there please *be* a time limit to grief? Some of us don't want to keep getting riddled with emotion every time we come across a hat or a letter or a thought.

Finding this hat today just reminded me that although I think I'm strong and together and with it, sometimes I can be truly weak and pathetic. Sometimes I can just melt into a ball of, not even depression, just a ball of emotion, and I just want to stay there and drown. Some days, it would just be so much easier to drown wouldn't it? To just give up and let all the emotion take you. The easy way out some would say. Why *shouldn't* we take the easy way out occasionally? Why do we always have to hold it all together? I have these two very different sides to me, and they contradict each other all the time. There's the me that's saying just wallow for once. Just slump on your sofa, stay in your dressing gown, fester in your own smell of not applying deodorant today, wallow and enjoy it. But then straight away, there's the other me. No, don't be so stupid, pick yourself up, pull yourself together and let's go go go. Put that emotion back in the box, shove it far away at the back of your mind and let's carry on with life. The thing is, I don't want to be *either* of these people. I don't want to sit and wallow and become a lifeless flump, eventually to be found half eaten by dogs. I don't want to just forget about my Dad and shove the emotion away and carry on. I want to be somewhere in between these two versions of 'me' and be able to feel the pain, deal with it and then let it go. I have a hard time letting emotions go after I've felt them. It's something I need to work on.

Finding my Dad's hat and smelling his smell still alive on it, set me back. It threw me into such massive emotion, that I didn't want to feel. Instead of feeling it, I just put it back in that box and put the hat away and came out of the bedroom and returned to happy strong mamma bear me. Really though, I need to learn to deal with the emotion so I can move forward. But then, what if he leaves me? What if I don't remember his smell anymore, or how he spoke, or the way he'd sing Bohemian Rhapsody at the top of his voice and call me 'Noddy' because all I used to do as a baby was sleep. Where's the in between? Does choosing full recovery mean I have to let all these years go and everything I know about myself and the way I deal with things go? Just like if I fully grieve and learn to let the pain of Dad's death go, does full recovery mean letting it all go? I'm not sure I'm ready for that yet. Leonie xox

November 2018 – Blog

I've just had my first counselling session and I did *not* enjoy it one bit. I knew what to expect because I've been on the other side as a counsellor in training, so I knew I'd get the head nods, the 'mmms' waiting for me to continue speaking and the long looks with silence. I knew it was coming and I'm fine with it, they're all useful tools in counselling but I did not enjoy talking about my childhood and then having silence for me to carry on talking. It's not like when I had CBT (cognitive behavioural therapy), where I was working with my CBT therapist to make actual progress. I was making plans and following workbooks and having to achieve little targets each week. I think as well, I was so apprehensive because I had *such* a good relationship with my CBT therapist. She was the first one I ever stuck to, I went to all my sessions (when I didn't have an anxiety attack and cancel (often!)) But I *wanted* to go, I wanted to participate, and I wanted to make changes to get better. That was because of her. She was such a massive influence on me and my life, and she really helped me change some things for the absolute better. I wish I'd had her so many years ago when everything started. With this session though, I didn't feel that 'click'. Although she is lovely, I found trying to fill the silence hard. I'm telling her about my eating disorder, I'm telling her about my religious upbringing, I'm telling her how trying to be perfect got the better of me. That's it. She asked how it all started. That's the summary of it... But she wanted more... What *more* was there to tell her? Then suddenly, I'm harping on about Dad killing himself, I say he's hanged himself, she makes a sad face, and then nods for me to carry on... What more is there to say, he's dead, I can't really expand on that can I. I think I'm going to find these sessions a challenge but I'm determined to see them through because I really do think they'll help. I've never really had the space to talk about the past. I think that's what I need to talk about, because it still impacts me today. Maybe if I talk about it all, I'll be able to breathe a bit better, feel a bit lighter, smile a bit wider. I hate talking about myself and more importantly, I hate having people focus and look at me. But I do believe it'll help so I want to give it a go. I told her I look like a tall, ugly, broad shouldered fat ogre and she said "is that how you see yourself?" with a disapproving look on her face and then started telling me there's nothing wrong with being tall and tutted at the ugly fat ogre bit. There may be nothing wrong with being tall, but it's how I *feel* so why did she then try and tell me that's not at all right… I'm feeling a little angry about the whole session and I don't know why. Recovery is hard. Leonie xox

November 2018 – Blog

Some questions I want to focus on and answer today. What is the 'perfect' body to you? I'm not sure there is a perfect body. We all want what we don't have, and the thing is, what's perfect to us, isn't perfect to the person who owns it. There's no perfect, it doesn't exist, we just unfortunately believe it does and can't get past that thought process. Are you a confident person? Some days, I can put on my best clothes and slap on a bit of makeup and put on my jewellery and I can feel amazing. I can look in the mirror and see past the size of me. I can look and just see me the person. Some days I can really look beyond my eating disorder and even my anxiety and I can see *me*. I can see a Mum to a beautiful baby. I can see someone who loves to study and who is *finally* starting her degree. I can see someone who loves tattoos, and someone who loves bright colourful hair. I can see someone who has many dreams, loves, hobbies, ambitions, but is too tired to pursue any of them. Some days, I can be as confident as a great white and other days I curl up into a ball, put on my largest hoodie, and hide away believing I am Shamoo the whale. Yesterday I was feeling a bit down, and while today I've had a great day so far with my best friend shopping, I came across two new songs that triggered off so much emotion in me. The first I heard in the car on the radio and it just made me feel sad. Jess Glynne, who is an amazing artist, sung 'Thursday' and the lyrics are so beautiful I thought I'd write them here.

"I'm tired of feeling so broken
I'm tired of falling in love
Sometimes I'm shy and I'm anxious
Sometimes I'm down on my knees
Sometimes I try to embrace all my insecurities
So I won't wear makeup on Thursday
'Cause who I am is enough…
I just wanna feel beautiful…"

These lyrics just got to me, it was exactly how I felt yesterday. I *am* tired of being anxious. I'm tired of feeling broken from the hurt of my divorce, my whole marriage, my Dad. I want to feel enough and yet I want to change so much about myself at the same time. I do just want to feel beautiful. It's like she was singing the song directly to me and it just got me choked up, but in a truly beautiful way. So then I searched for the song to download and I came across this next song, again by her. It's called 'Broken.' Now *this* song I interpreted a different way – read these lyrics then I'll explain.

"Sometimes when the day goes by
I've missed it because all I did was cry
You always know the reason why
You know me
You always got the words that never let me down, let me down
Always make me laugh somehow
You tell me don't worry
When I've done wrong
It's something that I'll never know
How you can love someone so broken…"

I know this song is probably talking about a loved one, helping them through but I interpret this song like the two versions of me I talked about the other day. I feel like sometimes when my eating disordered voice creeps in, as it has done, does and will do, there's always a bit of *me* in there, fighting back and this is me, these lyrics are the 'me' part. Sometimes my eating disorder takes me to a dark place, and sometimes I'll feel guilty for eating this, looking this way etc, as though I've done something wrong and I've failed, and I deserve to be punished. But the 'me' in there tells me it's OK. I understand the reason I feel like this, and I understand that I'm broken and bruised, but I still love me anyway. These lyrics remind me that when I lose my balance and can't breathe, just as she sings, I can still hold myself close, understand myself and *love* myself.

These lyrics are so powerful and so emotional, and these two songs are full of soul, beauty and purity and I love them. I think music helps in recovery so much. Leonie xox

November 2018 – Blog

My ex messaged me to tell me he's bought a new car with his girlfriend. I don't consider myself a bitter person, but I am absolutely fuming, and I am feeling bitter and hurt. My ex has never been good with money and while we were together, he borrowed countless amounts from me that never got paid back in full. He wasted his money on selfish and foolish things, and never spent it on us as a family, even when we didn't have Alissa. When Alissa was maybe five or six months, I can't remember exactly, his Mum sold her house and gave each of her children twelve grand. I later found out that six thousand pounds of that money was meant to be for me, but my ex insisted on his Mum giving him the full amount. He did not spend ONE PENNY on us as a couple or a family. We could have pulled our money together with that and put down a deposit. We could have got a family car instead of sitting in his horrible window cleaning van, unsuitable for a baby. We could have just done stuff as a family but no. So, what I find infuriating, is that if I had been given that six thousand, I would have saved it for Alissa, for her future. But not even one hundred pounds for Alissa's savings from her Dad. Instead, he goes and buys himself a racing toy which cost eleven grand. All the money on a toy he didn't use once. I think this is probably why I'm so upset, angry and emotional. He's happily gone and got himself a new family, and hey, six months into the relationship, bought a family car with her. I feel like my whole relationship was nothing. It meant nothing to him, fine, but what a waste for me. Why not just tell me after year one. Why drag it on for five years. Why hurt me so much. I can't describe the hurt. It's like tearing apart my heart and feeling every single rip and now this message just opened it all back up again.

Amongst all that though, I am so relieved and happy that I never have to have that feeling of insecurity with him, wondering which girl he's talking to, sending inappropriate pictures of himself to, wondering what he's hiding from me. Those days for me are over. So, although I was so upset last night, once I realised this and it hit me, that I *never* have to go through that pain again, I felt better. It's in the past and that's where it'll always be. Then I realised, I'm the one who's come out on top. I may have lost someone who didn't love me, but he lost someone who loved him more than anything in the world. Who is the real loser in this situation?

Leonie xox

November 2018 – Blog

Today I am braving the bus with Alissa (my BIGGEST FEAR) to meet a friend who lives about an hour away and then we're catching the train back to hers which is OK because she'll be with me. Later though, I'll have to catch the train home with Alissa by myself and I am very anxious about it. I'm sure we'll be OK and won't end up in Timbuktu, but the anxiety is definitely here, big and strong and won't leave me alone.

After the message from my ex about the car, I was feeling annoyed and hurt but I let Alissa go with him because I promised myself right from the beginning that I wasn't going to do any Jeremy Kyle nonsense of using my baby as a tool to get back at my ex. She absolutely adores him, and I know how important it is to have a good relationship with your Dad and I *want* her to have the BEST relationship with us both. She was due back at four o'clock and he messaged me saying she'd not had an afternoon nap, so I messaged him back saying OK, just make sure she's home *by* four-thirty because she'll be tired. I gave him an extra half an hour window because his side of the family never run on time. I got her dinner ready for four-thirty and he didn't bring her home until five-fifteen. I was standing at the kitchen sink so frustrated I was crying. They weren't even tears of sadness; it was pure frustration. I was *so* angry that my poor baby was so tired, and I had her dinner ready. I like to stick to a good bedtime routine with her. Dinner is always between four and five, then bath and bed for six o'clock. She came back too tired to eat and was falling asleep in the highchair. Any parent can empathise with how annoyed I was. As I stood at the kitchen sink, texting him with no reply (and before I hear you say, well he was driving of course he wouldn't reply – he *always* texts when driving). I was getting more worked up, anxiety kicking in and now I'm anxious because I know she'll be tired, anxious because where are they and why isn't he replying to my messages. Is she OK? Angry because her dinner is now cold. Angry because he's got a new car. Angry because I found out his car is still SORN so shouldn't be on the road, so he's got my baby in his illegally driven car. Angry because I'm ANGRY. I do something that I haven't done in a very long time and self-harm.

I haven't done this since my *very* early days of pregnancy, so we're talking when I was three weeks pregnant, and I found out at five weeks and stopped all destructive behaviours. For me, this is a huge thing. It's a reminder that although I'm OK, I'm *not* OK. A reminder that although a lot of my days are happy, when my anxiety kicks in I am *not* OK. A reminder that sometimes it's OK to *not* be OK. Leonie xox

November 2018 – Blog

I managed the bus well yesterday and didn't panic too much which I'm proud about and I had a truly lovely day. Then I had a major anxiety attack as I missed the train at four-thirty and the next one was at five o'clock, but I would have had to walk home which takes thirty minutes from the train station. It was pouring with rain, so I didn't know what to do. My friends Mum was at her house and kindly offered me a lift back to the town we originally met in so I could get the same bus home. I thought this would be better for my anxiety but obviously the traffic was so busy as it was rush hour and the train would have only taken ten minutes had I just been courageous. We didn't get to this town till gone five o'clock so it took half an hour to get there and I then started crying in the back seat, having a panic attack thinking about the rush hour traffic on a jam packed bus. My WORST nightmare... No wait, my worst nightmare is that but with Alissa screaming the whole way and being stuck in stand still traffic. Alissa WAS screaming in the car because she was so tired. Thank goodness my friends Mum obviously sensed I was super stressed and trying not to cry and she gave me a lift all the way home. I got in at five-twenty, rushed to do dinner but managed to get it all done and both in bed by six-twenty, only twenty minutes after bedtime. It was such a shame that my day ended badly, and the anxiety won me over because the whole day up until that point was really perfect. I was *so* proud of myself for catching the bus in the morning. I was so proud of myself for making the journey even though it was heavily raining and even though it was so out of my comfort zone. Alissa was so happy to see our friend, and she loved her day out. It's such a shame that anxiety snuck in and took me over completely just because I missed my train.

On another note, I've started restricting my calories again. I'm not one hundred per cent sure why, and it's not a super low restriction but I am very *aware* that I am heading back into restriction. It's all been triggered by this stuff with my ex. I'm just finding it so hurtful and hard. Everything feels difficult when it comes to him. Selfishly, I just wish he wasn't in our lives. Yesterday has drained me, physically and mentally and I'm finding recovery a choice I don't want to make today. Leonie xox

December 2018 – Blog

I wouldn't say I'm relapsing, but I'm getting those familiar feelings – I'm starting to get ridiculously frustrated going over my set limit, almost crying when I eat at my Mum's house (her house is a huge binge trigger for me.) I'm sat here now feeling a bit sick because I've been to Mum's this morning to help and eaten some stuff I didn't want to eat, and I just don't feel good. Mentally and physically. I'm typing it out to keep myself distracted from dwelling on how bad I feel. I've been so happy lately and have been really trying to stay positive and choose recovery every day but now Ethel has crept her way back in and she's really getting to me. I keep listening to triggering songs too which is *bad* for me. Music is so powerful for me and can really help me but can also really hinder me. I've got counselling tomorrow, and I'm not sure whether to mention all this there or not. Last time I went (that dreaded first appointment I talked about), she asked me if I wanted help for my eating disorder. I don't know how to answer that question. I desperately do but of course I also don't ever want to lose Ethel because she's powerful and she gives me control when I need it.

I was looking for a spare memory stick at my Mum's yesterday for a Christmas gift I'm putting together, and I came across Dad's memory stick which I gave to Mum because she needed one. It still has all his stuff on, and I found his 2016 suicide letter. He didn't leave one in the end, but he always drafted one up, every year, just in case. It made me sad. I felt sad reading it and sad thinking about it and just sad really. I'm trying to stay positive but it's hard when things keep unexpectedly coming up.

On a happier note, I absolutely *love* buying gifts for people. Nothing makes me happier than splashing my cash on the ones I love. I am therefore super excited about Christmas and

I can't wait to see the smiles on my friends faces. I can't wait for my Mum to see the Pandora earrings I've got, because they are, if I say so myself, stunning. I just can't wait to gift give and spread smiles. I think that's the best thing for me and my mental health. Making other people happy really does make me HAPPY.

I don't have anything else to say so now I just need to sit with these uncomfortable full feelings of over calorie eating and just let it BE. Ethel needs to know and understand that I am stronger. I do not need laxatives; I do not need to go and throw up right now. I do not need any of your horrible behaviours that just make me feel even worse. I just need to let this feeling pass. Leonie xox

December 2018 – Blog

I planned to write last night but I got distracted by an email from the Open University and when I came onto my student page, I saw that my course is now officially open, and I have my start dates. I am so excited to get started and use my brain again. I am a bit apprehensive because I have no idea what to do with Alissa. I investigated childcare yesterday and they all averaged around fifty pounds per *session*. Per session. So just for the morning it was fifty pounds of my non-existent money. I can't believe how expensive it is to have someone look after your little bundles of joy. I now have no idea what to do but I'm just going to do what I can and when she's two she'll be entitled to some free childcare which is great. She's not two till July so I am worrying how I'm going to cope until then, but I know I'll find a way.

My second session of counselling was an utter waste of time. My counsellor told me next time I'm feeling anxious waiting for Alissa's Dad to drop her home and he's late, to 'shake it out.' At which point, she physically got up out her chair and started shaking her body like she was performing a tribal weather dance. She also kept mentioning something, which, to one with an eating disorder, you probably shouldn't ever say. 'Take back control' was what she kept repeating to me. Now, she meant it in terms of still letting my ex have control over me, because he knows how anxious I'll get if he's late with Alissa so possibly uses this to control things (no idea if this is the case or not.) She meant it in a very positive and empowering way, like, go on girl, take back control... But obviously Ethel is here now so she has decided that yes, we will indeed take back control and we will show her who has the most control in all the world and enter eating disorder relapse brain.

I mentioned before to you chums that I'm scared to go over my set limit of calories and now I'm ridiculously annoyed that after days of barely eating I'm not losing anything (probably because my sleep deprived Shamoo the whale body is clinging onto every last ounce of fat.) So now I just feel cold, tired, grumpy and coffee has become my best friend once more. I feel like I can't stop now until I have my control back in life. Until everything stops sucking, and until for once in my life, things just become a little easier.

I have made a small step towards recovery with my anxiety though, because today I am officially catching *two*, yes, two busses, and I don't feel anxious. I feel like it'll be OK. Now that, for me, is a *massive* deal. Like truly massive. The train is still too scary to face but the bus – bring it on! Leonie xox

December 2018 – Blog

Some happy news finally. I wrote a while ago about receiving a letter saying a benefit I receive for being ill was stopping and I had a major anxiety attack trying to phone and get it sorted. Today I came home from my Mum's and checked my emails. I'm not sure whether it's been sorted out now, but I think it probably has. I've been back paid eight hundred pounds from money owed to me over the months. This has seriously lifted *such* a massive weight off my shoulders because now, even if they mess it all up and I don't have enough money for my rent and my bills, now I *do* have enough money for my rent and bills for at least one month. I'm so relieved. I can't tell you what a burden it's taken off my shoulders knowing I'll be able to afford my bills come January first. I hate not being able to afford things and I hate being worried and uncertain with money and not feeling like I've got any control over my finances. This, for me, is a massive WIN for today and I'm super pleased it's been sorted. I really hate money and the power it has in such a negative way. I hate that I can't give Alissa more and I hate that I can't just live without thinking about whether I'm going to have enough money to afford some more Heinz beans if they're not on offer for two pounds.

In other news, food is really getting to me now. I've gone over by fifty calories today, which the normal part of my brain is screaming that's nothing and to chill out. But obviously Ethel is laughing her head off in the background ready to punish me. It's only three o'clock in the afternoon. I'm annoyed and angry at myself. I hate that my eating disorder brings out anger in me. It's not an emotion I like, and I just need to stay focused on trying to reach little goals and make small steps because *any* steps we take for our recovery counts. Leonie xox

December 2018 – Blog

Dear Ethel, my eating disorder,

I decided to write this letter to you, to tell you what I *really* think of you. You see Ethel, when you first wrote to me, those twelve years ago, I thought you were going to be a great friend. You told me we'd be the best of friends, and that our relationship would last forever. You were right there.

What you didn't tell me though, was that you are spiteful and hateful. You are a bully and an abuser. You wrote to me and you masked yourself, and you made me believe that you were a bright light that I was walking towards. I looked at you Ethel, in those first few months of our ever-lasting relationship, and you were so positive. You had my back. I'm thankful to you for that. You gave me a feeling of great power and you made me feel as though I could do anything I wanted. You gave me control and I started looking and feeling better with you there. As the months went on though, you changed in colour, in size, shape, in everything. You started to get darker and darker. Your eyes became slanted and evil, showing nothing but the cold. The bright light around you that was holding my hand and leading me somewhere great disappeared, and all that was left was you. You made me go lower and lower until one day I just stopped eating.

I began to see your true colours and they were black Ethel, they were so very black. You came with a great depression that lasted in me a long time. You dragged me further and further down, pulling at my leg, knowing I couldn't shake you off. For someone so light, you became so very heavy and you sat on my chest reminding me every minute of the day that you were there. You bullied me for the smallest things. You constantly told me I wasn't good enough until one day you told me I was *nothing*. I looked in the mirror, and you were behind me, whispering mean things in my ear about myself. You took away any bit of self-confidence that I had and replaced it with fear and hatred of myself.

I began looking in the mirror five months later not knowing who was staring back. You started to take my personality away. Everything that made me, *me,* you began to steal and snatch. I thought I was smart because I worked so hard at school, but then you took that too. You just left me as a shell, and I didn't know how to *be* a shell. You started telling me I should do bad things to myself, that I'd feel much better after one slice on my skin with a blade, after one shove of the fingers down the throat, one inhale of the deodorant at the back of class. You started to hate me so much that you wanted me to hurt myself more and more. Friends don't do that Ethel, they just don't.

Then a year passed, and you were still there, and I tried to get rid of you Ethel. I told you I didn't want to be your friend anymore. I even told you I'd get help to get rid of you, but you stayed, like a bad smell, making my throat retch and burn. I wanted to destroy you, but you remained and now it's been twelve years and you're still here. Sometimes you're my very best friend and sometimes you're just an acquaintance in the background, every now and again popping up to say hello so I know you're still there.

I don't want to be your friend, but somehow, when you decide to be best friends again, I go along willingly, and I do everything you tell me to. I hope one day you'll respect my wishes and leave for good. I don't think you should be anyone's friend Ethel. You're not a nice person. I'm sorry to have to tell you the truth, but you're not kind and you're not my friend. But for now, you're here and I guess you'll stay for as long as you decide. Please Ethel, please just be a bit nicer to me this time. I'm not as young as I was then. Things are harder, I'm more tired and things are more difficult. But I'm trying. I promise, I'm trying to be your friend.

Just in case I don't get the chance to ever write again, what I really want to say to you is this. I wish I'd never met you. I hate you. You've taken away so much of myself and you've destroyed so many parts of my life. I wish you'd chosen someone else. It's selfish I know, but I wish you didn't pick me. I didn't ask you to come and be my friend. I didn't ask you to take over. Ethel, you really hurt me. Then, now and all the times in between. Ethel. Please. LEAVE ME ALONE.

Yours ever so kindly, Leonie xox

December 2018 – Blog

Here's a realisation I had this morning. I think it came from two things. Firstly, I had my counselling session yesterday, and yet again, it wasn't massively productive or helpful. She keeps asking what I want to bring to the session and I really don't know. Obviously when I first asked for the counselling I needed to talk about Dad, it was bubbling over, my grief, my need to talk about it, and then to talk about everything in my past. But after waiting four months for the counselling to come through, I feel like I've found this space, where I talk to you all. So now I don't really know what to say on my weekly Tuesday sessions. That aside, we briefly spoke about my ex yesterday and she kept saying she could see how much he'd hurt me. That surprised me a little, because I suppose I'm so used to making jokes about him, us, about the whole situation, and pretending it doesn't bother me in the slightest. To have someone see that actually the things he's done have hurt me and broken me, is surprising to me. Then, I started watching a three-part drama on BBC iPlayer last night called "Mrs Wilson". If you haven't watched it, I strongly recommend it, it's brilliant. Mrs Wilson, who loses her husband in the first episode, finds out immediately after, that he has another wife and child... I won't say too much more as there are a few twists and turns but I finished the last episode this morning whilst jogging on the spot (I know, I am *that* annoying person.) The ending was a big wake up call for me. After yet another blow, it jumps to three years later, where she is in a Nunnery or somewhere similar. So, it jumps to three years later and she's in this place and here it is. She's found PEACE. All that's happened to her, all that he put her through *after* his death, where she couldn't face him for an explanation, where she had to find everything out and handle that level of emotion towards him without him actually being there. While still feeling grief for the husband she loved and lost, but whilst feeling all the other emotions that come with finding out your husband is a liar and a cheat. She went through all of that and the outcome is that she finds PEACE. This is a true story, I forgot to mention, so this is a true account of what happened. She found God and that led her to peace.

Now, I'm not saying we all need to go and find God to find inner peace but after I finished the episode and my on the spot jog, I went into the bathroom to wash my face and this is where the realisation hit me. I realised that I didn't ever **need** my ex-husband. All this time I've been thinking that I *needed* him, that I was nothing without him, that he gave me the world and everything in it. All this time I've been deluding myself that I wasn't capable of anything, because everything I accomplished, *he* gave me, or allowed me or encouraged me. I have been carrying this feeling around that I was nothing without him and that I couldn't be independent without him.

Today I realised, I *NEVER* needed him. I wanted him. I adored him. I loved him. But I didn't need him. Now I've realised it, I feel SO much lighter. I am smiling again because I know that I can do *whatever* I want to in life. I know that I was always strong, even when he made me weak. That's why we didn't succeed. I was never that weak girl. He thought I was. I thought I was. But I never was. *THAT* is my recovery for today. Realising that I was always, that I am, MORE. Leonie xox

December 2018 – Blog

I want to talk today about being a Mum and where it all started with my birth. I had a horrific birth in the end, after a day and a half of contractions, I was rushed from my lovely calm birthing room, where I'd planned and hoped to have a water birth, to the emergency birthing room where they can monitor baby. Then, whilst in that room, I pushed for an hour and a half and after no joy delivering, was rushed to emergency theatre, where I had emergency forceps and an episiotomy. It was the complete opposite to what I wanted, and it was truly horrific, with bleeding in theatre afterwards. I was speaking to another Mum who had the exact same birth as me and she was saying she was finding it hard to process her birth and she felt she didn't receive the proper care she needed. I can really relate to this because I really did feel it was a traumatic birth and I wasn't cared for afterwards properly. My birth has massively impacted my decision that I don't ever want any more children.

I think it's important to talk about these things. The more I think about it, it *was* a traumatic event that I had to go through and deal with. As the months went by, the memory of the birth became just that, a memory. The pain faded, the stitches healed, and I even had sex again. I feel deeply for the mums out there who have such negative birthing experiences and then are just made to feel they can't talk about them because they have the beautiful baby, so what's there to complain about. For ALL aspects of our mental health, it's important that we SPEAK out and talk about these things. These *feelings*. I hope there's a Mum, perhaps a new Mum, who is reading this and thinking actually yes, my birth wasn't what I'd planned and it has made me feel *xyz* and I *do* want to talk about how I'm feeling with someone.

On another note, yesterday my ex said he wanted Alissa Christmas Eve to take her to see the reindeers with his girlfriend and her son and it genuinely made me feel emotional and sad. Not because he's going with his new partner, but because the thought of them playing happy families with *my* child really grates on me. I find it so hard to cope with the fact that they take her out and act as though Alissa is their child. I don't want her to go, but I promised myself I'd never use Alissa as a pawn. I know she'd love it, and she loves her Dad so much. She'd love the day out and it's selfish of me to not let her go. I'm having a hard time dealing with it and that's OK, just so long as I acknowledge those feelings and don't let them be another reason for relapse.

Today I had a lovely drink with a good friend along the beach earlier. I walked Alissa an hour early and she slept for the hour and I sat and looked at the beach and the waves and felt a beautiful peace. It was healing to walk along and think how fortunate I am, and how blessed I am. To think of Dad and smile through the pain. To think of Grandad. To think of the hurt I've felt through all these things, but how lucky I am to be here, today, with Alissa by my side. When my friend came into the pub, we had a lovely conversation which led onto talking about her previous marriage and divorce. I asked her how she has forgiven her ex-husband after being hurt so badly by him. She told me she's forgiven him completely and that there is no bitterness left and that it came when she found her happiness again. It just got me thinking. I don't know *why* I feel so bitter towards my ex. I don't have any romantic feelings for him anymore. That's all gone. I don't even know if there's hurt left. When he's here, as he is now, doing the bedtime routine with Alissa, he makes her laugh and she's so happy with him. At first, I roll my eyes, and feel annoyed that he makes her so happy. But then I stop and think and wonder *why.* Why do I feel this horrible bitter feeling towards him? Why don't I want Alissa to be with him on the weekend spending quality time with her Dad and making similar memories that I made with my Dad? I don't understand why I feel bitter. I truly don't. A small part of me feels hurt that he moved on so quickly and that I was just the 'go between', from the former love of his life, to his current. I was just a five year stop gap. I suppose the hurt is there. I really want to move on and find peace and just be friends with him, but I can barely look at him. He makes me so angry and so annoyed and full of hate. I don't know why, and I wish it would go. Leonie xox

January 2019 – Blog

Christmas was hard, and I had to really have a stern talking with myself in order to enjoy my food for the day. I felt better knowing what I was eating because I had a salmon fillet and my Mum is very good with veg and potatoes and cooks them well, with hardly any oil which is a *big* fear food for me. Sitting down and eating the meal was difficult but I'm just glad that the actual food was food I feel comfortable eating. It made things a lot easier. Alissa absolutely loved the day of course and I'm so surprised with how well she survived without a nap. She loved all her presents and was of course, thoroughly spoilt by my Mum, as was I. It was a lovely relaxing day, and for the first time in years, I didn't have to worry that my ex wasn't enjoying himself and wanted to go home and drink. I was just relaxed. It was nice. I think good days make such a difference in recovery because they make you *want* to recover. They make you want to put the effort in and move forwards. I feel ready to just move forwards. Ethel doesn't want to leave me, but I want her gone and that's a small, but significant step in recovery today. Leonie xox

January 2019 – Blog

Today I finished an essay that's been driving me crazy the last few days. I haven't been able to get my head around the essay question but then today it just started flowing and I completed it, three words below the word count. I feel a bit lighter mentally now, and it's one less thing to focus on. I am trying to get as much work done as I have an operation coming up in February and the recovery is going to be long and hard.

Ethel is back and my calorie limit has gone low again. I know there will always be periods of recovery and relapse. What's important is knowing and understanding that this won't be forever and that I've come out of it before and I will this time. Life is always about those small steps of recovery. It's important not to forget that. Some days I wonder if Ethel is really a mental illness because she's such a normal part of my life now when she reappears in force. But I need to remember that she IS an eating disorder and that does mean I have a serious mental illness. Eating disorders are *not* made up. They are not fun. It is not a case of simply eating. Above all, they are not for attention. A common misconception. It's no fun to feel extreme hunger pains, dizziness, cold all the time, headaches, no energy, no life, just because some people think we merely want a bit of attention. We each are different and our reasons behind how this illness started are all different too. Sure, it might be nice for some of us at some points to get a bit of TLC, just as anyone who is sick would like now and again. But do we do this just for a laugh... No. Because it's not a laughing matter. It's not fun lying down and feeling your bones and hating it but loving it at the same time. It's not fun to feel so rubbish all the time but have to pretend to everyone that you're happy. That you're alive. That you're OK. It's not fun to brush your hair and see too much hair on the brush and know that what you're doing is slowly killing you, but you can't do anything about it. You *can't* do anything about it. You'll never know that unless you develop an eating disorder but it's a feeling so deep you can never claw out or away from it. You can't ***just*** stop. You can't ***just*** eat. It's never as simple as that.

Today I almost took a bite out of a biscuit. Just one bite. I had to throw the whole pack away. They were my baby's gluten free biscuits, but the extreme fear that I might weaken and eat outside my 'allowed' petrified me. Then it hits you. It might be midday; it might be during the night. You realise you have a problem but you're not willing to get help for it. You realise that a two-calorie mushroom fills you with dread. You realise that you sliced your skin because you ate twenty calories over your limit for the day. You hate yourself. You can't stand to look in the mirror. You know that it's wrong, but you can't keep that food inside your body, so you do *whatever* it takes to get rid of it. You realise that things aren't OK. That you're not OK and you break. You break and crack on the inside and you just want the ground to swallow you, because you *can't* swallow.

What started out one innocent day as choosing to diet, choosing to just be healthier, choosing to lose a bit of weight, turns into something you can't choose and can't control. You cry and cry and cry because you're broken, and you'll never be fixed. Leonie xox

February 2019 – Blog

Where I've felt myself slip into relapse, I haven't had much to say on recovery. It's been over a month and I'm at a place now where I just want to be 'normal'. A month and a half with

Ethel making me low restrict and I've truly had enough. I long to eat three healthy meals a day and be done without a second thought. I'm desperate to not feel fear when a plate of food is put in front of me. More than that, I want to be able to eat in front of people without feeling such extreme guilt and shame. I promised myself that this year was going to be my year. I vowed to myself that I'd let all that's happened go and finally find peace and happiness. I told myself that this was the year I stopped being afraid to get out into the world and live my life with Alissa. I want these things to come true and I know they can't if I'm relapsing. So, this is where I draw the line. I've got five weeks left of recovery from surgery. During these five weeks I will probably stay in my relapse because I can't move around much so eating less is my only comfort that I won't gain heaps of weight. But when I'm physically back to my full strength that's the time. I'm ready to start my journey towards health again. I'm ready to build myself up and get strong, mentally. I'm done with beating myself up over a biscuit. I'm done crying because I ate one hundred calories over my goal for the day.

I'm done with letting Ethel rule my life like she's a Queen and the only important thing I have going for me. I have news for you, I'm the one in charge and I deserve to be happy. I deserve to pick up my fork and EAT. I deserve to LIVE. This is important for us all. Relapse is so horrible, but do you know what. It's not going to last. It's not going to win. Because we deserve to eat guilt free. So, whatever you must do to get to this place, where you're done and ready to build yourself back up, do it. Your happiness and your worth are important. Don't let your eating disorder take them away.

One day I'm going to be eating disorder relapse free for a whole year. That's a big goal for me but I'm going to make that happen because I deserve one year without this voice in my head draining me. It all starts with one day and one choice. One small step of bravery to decide that you are more important than I̲t̲. My day is coming. Leonie xox

February 2019 – Blog

It's eating disorder awareness week, so I just wanted to say that if you're like me, and decades into this disorder, then use this week to remind yourself where you started and how far you've come. Share your story because eating disorders love nothing more than to fester off you in the dark, alone and in secret.

Even though being seventeen at college was my first glimpse at what recovery could be like, it wasn't easy, and challenges did arise. At a Halloween party that year, a boy I liked pinned me down whilst we were alone and tried to have sex with me. I was tipsy, and I couldn't get him off and, in that moment, I was petrified. His weight on top of me made me feel as though I couldn't breathe, and if my friend hadn't walked in, I don't know how far he'd have gone. Although trauma will arise during all stages of both relapse and recovery, it's important to not give in.

Use this week to shout loud and shout proud. Recovery will only happen if you start using your voice to express your emotions instead of controlling food to supress them. Use this week to be kinder to yourself, use it to remind yourself of your journey. Let's make this a positive week. Maybe *It* is winning the battle right now... But don't let eating disorders win the war. Leonie xox

February 2019 – Blog

Today, I made another small step in recovery for my anxiety. I went on a date. That's right, you heard me. I almost cancelled but I didn't. I forced myself to go. I put on a bra that fully supported my breasticles, instead of one of those mum bras I usually wear, and I put on actual clothes and went for coffee. Sure, it was just coffee. But the point is, I pushed myself beyond what I felt comfortable with and did it anyway. The date itself was fine, but no sparks my end. I came home, however, feeling *good*. You know how I like to have these little realisations that hit me in life, well today I had another. This time eating disorder related. I think I've realised why this relapse has been difficult. When I first developed my eating disorder, it was fuelled by a self-hatred, a loathing of myself, so deep and raw that it burned my core. Over the years, that self-hatred lessened, and a self-love I never knew possible, emerged.

Fast forward to present day, and through all the ups and downs that have happened of late; from losing Dad and feeling terrible guilt for never being there for him, to divorcing a man I thought would never hurt me, because I could never have imagined hurting him. To going through a traumatic birth with Alissa and struggling with such a massive weight gain. These things gave me highs and lows, but through all of them, my self-love never really went away. If anything, after leaving my husband, I realised even more, the person I am, the person I want to be. It's been a year since I left my husband and I'm happier than ever before. I have a confidence back that I lost somewhere in our years of hurt and lies. What I've truly realised, perhaps today more than any other, is that I do, in fact *love myself*. I am absolutely, without a question of a doubt, one marvellous human being, with *so* much to offer this world. I will reach every single one of my goals, because I am strong, I am brave, and I am a warrior. I will not give up, and I will always show up, to give the best I can. This realisation today of how much self-love and care I have for myself has made me also realise why this relapse has been hard. I don't hate myself anymore. It's harder to starve when you don't hate yourself. This has contributed to feelings of failure and disappointment in myself for each day I don't stick to my calorie limit, but ultimately, I don't beat myself up about it for too long anymore. I move past it. I breathe and I let it all go. Today I've felt *fantastic* and I've felt like I've truly won at life today. Leonie xox

March 2019 – Blog

I'm struggling, not so much with eating foods, but with the feelings I get from eating them. I'm getting more and more annoyed and frustrated with myself for eating this or eating that. I'm feeling more and more like a failure every day I eat foods outside my 'safe' food items.

I'm still able to look in the mirror and feel happy with what looks back. I still feel confident and 'me' when I'm in my nice clothes, ready for the day ahead. It's just when I eat, I feel awful. Although I am finding the physical act of eating for the most part, OK, *how* I feel when I eat is getting worse. I think my point is – there are *so* many different, tiny little aspects of eating disorders that people don't think about. You might look at someone with an eating disorder and think they don't look like they have an eating disorder because they're out eating lunch with you. But you don't know what's going on in their head. You don't know what it took to get them there. You don't know the mental strength it takes to put that fork in your mouth for EVERY SINGLE BITE. There's SO much to an eating disorder. It's like an onion. Layers and layers of tears, layers and layers of depth.

So, I realised that ninety-nine per cent of why I feel so GOOD today is because it's twelve-thirty in the afternoon and I still haven't eaten. I ate quite a lot yesterday (an amount of calories I wasn't happy with) and so to 'punish' myself today, I decided last night I wouldn't eat till four o'clock. Then my calories for today would be low with what I've planned to eat. So, I feel GOOD because I'm sticking to it. I'm winning, I'm not failing. Being able to acknowledge this and self-reflect on it is helpful because now I realise that this isn't the way to feel good about myself. My day and my happiness and my positivity should *not* be determined by how much or little I eat. It's something I need to work on massively, but the fact is, I've realised it today and that, for me, is a very tiny, but still significant, step to my recovery. Leonie xox

March 2019 – Blog

There are so many hard choices we must make with an eating disorder, that can seem so easy to someone who's mentally healthy in that area of their lives. Like, when it comes to deciding whether to pick up the fork. When it comes to agreeing to go out to a family meal. When it comes to making any kind of choice. For 'normal' people, those who have a healthy relationship with food and their body, these choices may seem so small, unimportant and maybe even petty. Sure, if you haven't seen your family for months and you really want to see them, you may think "of course you'd say yes to going out." But what if, just what if, although you so desperately want to see them, you are more than petrified of the meal. Of making the CHOICE whether to pick up the fork, order what you want, or order what you know has the lowest calories. Eat the whole plate, or just eat half. Lose control or keep control. For those of us who suffer with an eating disorder, those choices are MASSIVE. Although we love our family, and want to go and see them, the intense fear of that family meal, means we lie and say we're ill and can't make it. It all comes down to CHOICES. For some of us, those choices are too hard. They drain our minds and our souls and suck the joy out of us. Choices are hard work and we must work extra hard, every day, to make the choice between health, happiness and recovery or 'control', feeling 'safe' and staying 'on track'.

Recovery is hard work, and making choices is a massive part of it. We should constantly remind ourselves that we are worth more than this disease, and that we deserve recovery. We deserve to make a carefree choice, based on love and happiness, not on what our eating disorders want for us. We deserve to have a healthy relationship with body and food, and we deserve to feel love and be loved for who we are. We are more than a number looking up at us. We are more than a food scale. We are more than the scales in our bathroom. We are more than we could ever imagine. Leonie xox

March 2019 – Blog

I want to talk about depression, on its own, as a massive mental illness for many people. I feel very blessed that I no longer suffer from the crippling thoughts and feelings depression brings, and I owe this completely to my darling baby girl, for helping me to find my wings and fly. But I can remember vividly the pain and burning desire to leave this world, like it was just yesterday. I think my depression came before my eating disorder, but I didn't know what it was yet. I remember very slowly feeling as though I was tumbling, further and further into a big black hole of emptiness, with no way to claw myself out. I was so worried about failing my G.C.S.E's – by failing I mean not getting my predicted As and A*s (which I didn't anyway because of Ethel). I felt this enormous pressure to not let anyone down, thinking that if I didn't get the best results, I would somehow disappoint everyone who knew me. I don't think anyone gave a care in the world about what grades I got really. The adults knew G.C.S.E's weren't the be all and end all of life but didn't think to tell me this little secret. I thought that if I didn't get the best results everyone would see that really, I was nothing special and just nothing in general, I guess. Ethel came along shortly after these feelings started creeping in and she worked with the depression to truly make me hate every bit of myself. But we're not here to talk about Ethel today (so get back in your cave you miserable tramp).

I remember watching Hollyoaks during my teens, and the song 'Breathe Me' by Sia came on at one point and it perfectly represented how I was feeling. I'd play it over and over in my bedroom, crying, self-harming, and wishing that I'd go to sleep and never wake up. There didn't seem to be anything to live for anymore. I didn't *want* to live for anything. I was so done, and so ready to escape this cruel world, and be at 'peace.' I somehow thought that if I killed myself, I'd be free from everything that was swallowing me whole. There would be days where I'd clutch at my heart and cry so much that I almost ran out of breath. Tears would stream down my cheeks and I longed for the pain to just go away. I didn't know *why* I was in so much pain, or *why* I felt so broken. I think that's the best word to describe the feeling. BROKEN. With no idea why you feel that way. It's a feeling so much greater than sadness, but you don't know why it's there. Nothing has happened, nobody has died, you haven't been through some horrific abuse or suffered a major trauma. You feel shattered and broken and your heart physically hurts but you don't understand why. Your thoughts just seem to get darker every day and that burning feeling that you need to just escape your body, your mind and your life, won't go away. You feel like you're slipping and maybe there's one or two hands trying to grab you and reach out to you, but you can never EVER seem to hold on to them. You just slip. Further and deeper and the crying is more uncontrollable than ever. Some days you can't cry because you have nothing left to give. Some days you don't even remember getting from a to b, from History to Maths, from home to school or work, from one room to another. Then other days, you feel everything. Every second is broken down into a thousand little pieces, and time doesn't seem to move. You just want to move but everything is stuck and you're not getting anywhere at all and you just want to move, so this feeling goes, passes, MOVES.

Depression boils down to screaming inside, to cutting yourself or burning yourself or any of the other hundreds of ways to self-harm, just to *feel* something other than the pain inside your **soul**. Depression is feeling everything in the world, all the pain, all the screams, all the burning. To then feeling absolutely nothing. To being a shell, empty, waiting for something to come inside and bring you to life. To feeling any of the thousand places in between nothing and everything. Depression can be masked and hidden deep inside someone, who may look so happy on the outside, but who is screaming out for help and care on the inside.

I don't know how I escaped that hole. I know Alissa pulled me out. But she didn't recover for me. I did that. I got better and I don't know when my depression truly lifted away but I haven't felt like that for a very long time. Depression is such a vile monster of a mental illness, and absolutely nobody deserves to suffer. More than that, nobody deserves to think that the world would be better without them in it. Nobody deserves to think that dying is better than living. Dying is NEVER better than living. There's a way out. I can't tell you how, I can't stop you slipping out of the hands that are trying to pull you up, but I can tell you, that there is a way. I'm proof. Leonie xox

March 2019 – Blog

Today I made a significant step in my personal recovery. I deleted my account for an eating disorder forum I was signed up with where you post and answer posts and get support from other people who are going through something similar. This was NOT a 'pro ana' site, I don't condone those. All the replies to people asking for advice on there were always to be healthy, go slow and steady, don't put yourself in danger etc. It was a loving and supportive community both in general and for me personally. However, I had an accountability on there where I'd post what I'd eaten, calorie intake, weight etc, to try and keep myself 'on track' and I realised today that if I'm to ever have any hope of a FULL recovery, then I can't be a part of communities like that, because they fuel my desire to be the best. So, I deleted it. I deleted my posts, my existence in that little loving world of people who are struggling as I am. I feel a little sad, but I know that for my recovery and for my SELF, I needed to let it go. Because, sometimes, the bravest thing you can do is say NO. Leonie xox

April 2019 – Blog

I want to talk about anxiety today. Often, doctors will diagnose a patient with both anxiety and depression together, with the anxiety, quite often being GAD (generalised anxiety disorder). While it's great to have a diagnosis that can lead to additional support and help, I find that often grouping the two together, means they don't get the care and attention they need, as separate mental illnesses. I've talked about depression as an illness, on its own, so now I'm talking about anxiety. Anxiety is a significant mental illness, and one that plagues my life daily. As I said in my post on depression, I am very fortunate not to suffer from that black hole of despair anymore. However, my anxiety – which, if we're talking professional diagnosis, is both social anxiety and GAD, is here every day.

Sometimes I think that I'm OK because if I go to places I know, or if I'm with people I feel safe around, I'm just like any other mentally healthy person. Of course, because these are the situations I mostly put myself in, I can feel quite anxiety free each day. That leaves me wondering if I really do have anxiety, because I'm 'OK' when I just have to pop to the shops, or go round my Mum's house or go out with my best friend.

(I feel safe with her because she drives and I know she would always bring me back if I felt anxious and she wouldn't take me anywhere outside of my 'safe' zones, unless I asked).

The thing I've come to learn about anxiety is that it can be there all the time, or it can come and go when it chooses. My anxiety is the latter. Here are a few examples of my anxiety this week alone. On Monday I wanted to take Alissa to a park we hadn't been to before. I know where it is, I've walked to that area before, but I've never actually been in the park itself. My anxiety kicked in – what if I'm imagining where the park is and it's not actually there? What if people look at me and wonder why I'm just walking my baby down here? What if we get to the park and Alissa needs her nappy changed? What if we get to the park and there are teenagers playing around and smoking and shouting and I don't feel safe? What if Alissa cries the whole walk there? What if it starts raining? What if I see someone I know and I'm all sweaty from the walk? What if? What if? WHAT IF? Best not go, best to just stay at home where it's safe and warm and dry. OK... We're staying in today! That was Monday, Thursday went like this;

Mum - "Are you coming to the meeting?" **6pm**

Me - "What time do you leave? **6:10pm**

Mum - "6.40." **6:10pm**

Me - "Oh I don't know, that's not really enough time to get me and Alissa dressed and sort everything out" **6:15pm**

Mum - "OK, just let me know. You just need to put a skirt on, you can do it." **6:25pm**

In the ten minutes it took for Mum to reply to that last message, I had worked myself up into a panic – it's six-fifteen, I only have twenty-five minutes, what if Alissa cries all evening? Seven to nine o'clock is a long time, she is usually asleep by eight o'clock, she'll be screaming while we're all meant to be quiet, I don't think it's a good idea. But I could give it a try, she did have a later nap, I'm sure she'll be OK. But she probably won't be. She'll be grizzly. It'll be nine-thirty by the time we're home, ten o'clock by the time she's asleep... But she might have a lie in. I'm sure she'll be OK... I don't know if it's a good idea.

Mum - "Are you coming?" **6:35pm**

Me - "You've given me five minutes to decide, I can't get ready in time now! No, I don't think I can do it. I'm sorry. I don't know. I want to but..."

That's just two examples of anxiety this week. Anxiety comes in all shapes and sizes. Sometimes it's 'what if' but sometimes it's just because there's not enough time to mentally prepare, the situation has been sprung on you, you don't feel safe. Going out on Thursday evening would have meant I was outside, not in bed with Alissa, safe and warm. I like to feel safe in the evenings and be at home. Anxiety, for me personally, means that I can't do things that others would love. I can't just say YES to an impulse BBQ on a Saturday evening, at a friends' house or down the beach. I can't just take Alissa out and GO somewhere, without hours of thinking, planning, deciding. Anxiety doesn't always win and a lot of the time, I *do* push myself to get out the house because Alissa is my motivation. But anxiety is a MASSIVE mental illness all on its own, and I think we all need to understand this and learn more about it. It doesn't just coexist with depression. It's not a fake illness. It's real and it decides every day whether you stay cooped up in your safety or whether you push yourself out and meet a goal you really want to achieve. Anxiety is a monster, a silent, evil monster, and a lot of the time, I loathe it more than my eating disorder. My recovery isn't just around food and body image. It's around anxiety too because getting rid of anxiety for me, would be such a massive thing. It would mean I could live carefree with Alissa, without worrying that she's gone for the day with her Dad and he's not going to apply sun cream. It would mean I wouldn't have a panic attack because Alissa is walking in the garden and I can see where she might trip over and hurt herself. It would just mean *freedom.* Leonie xox

April 2019 – Blog

Today I went out with my best friend and I ate unexpectedly, taking me way over my calorie limit. I felt OK about it as I was having so much fun but when I went back to my Mum's to pick Alissa up, a comment was made about how I 'pick' at foods (which I do), but it just made me *so* emotional. I had to just leave. I don't have an open relationship with my family when it comes to my eating disorder, so I can't talk about my feelings surrounding food, but I wanted to scream

"Maybe if you'd all helped and supported me twelve years ago, I wouldn't have a problem and pick at food. Maybe if you'd encouraged me to find food freedom and supported me on the journey I wouldn't always pick food apart when I come over and search the cupboards for food to eat... MAYBE IF YOU'D JUST ALL HELPED ME I WOULDN'T STILL HAVE AN EATING DISORDER TWELVE YEARS LATER!"

I obviously said none of the above, but when I got home, I just wanted to cry. I'm now sat feeling guilt ridden at how much I've eaten today, deciding whether to take laxatives tonight and feeling utterly rubbish all because of one comment.

Although I feel like this, I still forced myself to make my fruit and yoghurt for dinner, because I wanted to eat something that felt healthy today. I felt physically sick eating this, and I didn't finish it all. But the point is, even though I didn't want to eat it, and it's taken me way up and over any calorific comfort zone, at least I still gave it a go. At least I still pushed myself to do it. I'm sitting feeling full, uncomfortable, guilty, sick, and like I want to fast tomorrow and never eat again. But at least I know that even if comments are made against me about food, I can still do *my* best to try and make steps towards recovery.

I'm so sick of this disease, but more than that, I'm so sick of pretending I don't still have this illness to my family and not talking about it. Why don't they ever want to talk about it and *help me.* Leonie xox

May 2019 – Blog

To the fifteen-year-old me,

To the fifteen-year-old me who used to come home from school and cry in her bedroom because she didn't feel like she had anything to live for. To the fifteen-year-old me, who so desperately wanted to be at peace and felt like suicide was the only way to ever accomplish this. To the fifteen-year-old me, who felt only a black hole inside her, and who could never get to the top and climb out. To the fifteen-year-old me, who felt like if she failed her exams, everyone would know she was a fake and a failure and not worth anything at all.

To the fifteen-year-old me, who decided one day she would start starving, because that way, she would have 'control' over her life. To the fifteen-year-old me, who thought slicing her skin open and watching herself bleed was the only way she'd ever really know she was still alive on this earth. To the fifteen-year-old me, who didn't know why she was here and who could only cry repeatedly. To the fifteen-year-old me, who floated around school in a daze, hoping to drop dead. To the fifteen-year-old me, who felt everything and nothing all at the same time, and who was screaming so deeply on the inside, waiting for someone to hear her cries. To the fifteen-year-old me, your heart hurt for a long time and you didn't deserve any of the pain you suffered. To the fifteen-year-old me.

I'm sorry for what I put you through. I'm sorry I hurt you. I'm sorry I didn't allow you the space to grow and I'm sorry I interfered with your childhood body and didn't trust it to figure everything out all by itself. I'm sorry I starved you, cut you, stuck my fingers down your throat, over exercised till you fainted, and I'm sorry that I didn't realise your worth. But, throughout it all, you SURVIVED. I promise from now, to love you, to cherish you, to see your worth, your beauty and your value in this world. Above all, I promise to get better and to recover. For the young girl I abused for so long, who was screaming out for help, but who, throughout all, came out shining. It's finally time.

And to the twenty-seven-year-old me now. I'm sorry I am still starving you. I'm sorry I still suffer with this horrible disease. I'm working on it. I promise.

Yours then, now and always, Leonie xox

May 2019 – Blog

There's a big part of me that still wants to lose another stone, so I can finally be back to my lowest weight. There's a big part of me that doesn't want to keep eating because if I do, I'll 'get fat'. There's a big part of me that doesn't want to get better, because if I do, I'll lose something I've had with me for twelve years. There's a big part of me that fears food, of swallowing, of it being in my body. There's SO MANY BIG PARTS OF ME THAT ARE SCARED TO DO THIS. But there are so many more reasons why I *should* do this and why I want to do this. I don't want to end up in inpatient one day because I've gone too far, and I no longer get the freedom of choice. I don't want to faint ever again. I don't want to feel ill anymore. I don't want to lose my hair, feel cold and tired all the time and constantly dizzy. I don't want to feel slogged down with water instead of food. I don't want to do this anymore. I don't want to hurt my body and my mind anymore. I want to be FREE. Leonie xox

May 2019 – Blog

I feel like recovery just goes around in circles. I feel like I'm always trying to recover, and I always just end up back in relapse. I don't know what kind of flow I should be following; I don't know what foods to eat, I don't know how much I should eat etc... I feel like I don't know what to do now, what to focus on. Even though I'm the expert of my body and my disorder, I feel lost. I think my point is, that for full recovery I feel I need some kind of support, help and guidance. That's hard for me, because so far, the help I've had from professionals has been rubbish.

I don't know what to do with myself. I'm eating more regularly, but now I need to eat *more*. How do I do that? Do I just eat some biscuits? Do I eat some chips? Do I eat EVERYTHING until I don't WANT to eat everything? How do I find this *food freedom* that so many people are going on about? I know there is no right or wrong approach to recovery, and it's about taking small steps every day. But what if, no matter how many small steps you take, you never get there? That's how I feel today and I don't *want* to recover today. I just want to stay disordered because at least I know what I do with my disordered eating. I have *no* clue how to do recovery eating and recovery as a whole and it's scary. Leonie xox

May 2019 – Blog

Today I am talking about the bread roll. Yesterday, I made a *huge* step in recovery and picked up a round bread roll from the fresh bakery aisle. Now I *never* allow myself to buy crusty bread rolls or French stick. Don't ask me why, I just don't. Usually if I want something outside of my allowed, safe, disordered foods, it takes me sometimes up to an hour to decide whether to finally pick up the item or leave it. I often pick something up, walk around with it, go put it back. Repeat the cycle. Or, if you're a lucky customer nearby, you may see me pick it up and put it down over and over again whilst standing in the same spot. My brain really messes with me when I'm out shopping, and buying things not on my list, or that I know I 'shouldn't' (or what my disorder *tells* me I shouldn't) have, is *really* hard. So, for me, picking up that bread roll was amazing and I'm super proud I did it.

Yesterday was a bad day for me. I ate too much food, and just allowed myself a bit of freedom which initially was great. The morning started off well and although I'd eaten more than usual, I felt OK. I felt like my body just needed a break from low calorie stuff, but by the evening, the guilt crept in. The eating disorder won over the recovery brain that was feeling good. Ethel is *such* a bully and she came in force and I ended my night by taking laxatives because I felt so ashamed and *guilty* for eating so much more than my allowed calorie intake and my allowed foods. I then felt like maybe I should just give this recovery stuff up. Maybe it's not for me? Maybe it's better to just stay in disordered eating – restrict and then every now and again let myself enjoy nice foods that I never allow myself to eat. I felt like it would just be so much easier to just stay with what I know. I've been in this restrictive eating disordered hell for longer than a decade, and at least I *know* it and so I'm not surprised by it. But then I thought WAIT. Hold on there a moment and take a breath – recovery IS going to be hard. Recovery IS going to be unknown. Recovery for me, is hard, because I don't know how I'm going to feel one day to the next, because my feeling of achievement and success and happiness all relates to how little I eat. OF COURSE this is going to be a hard journey. Does that mean I should give up and stay in such a horrible place with food? NO WAY. I need to STOP linking my emotional happiness on whether I've starved myself all day long. The two do NOT go together. Positive feelings and starving are NOT linked, and my self-worth and self-love do NOT come from whether I've managed to not eat all day.

That's a tough feeling and goal for me but it's something I've just realised. I've also just realised that I think the reason I never get through recovery and stick at it, is because when I eat, I feel like I don't have my eating disorder, *because* I'm eating more so then I panic, because deep down, a part of me still NEEDS my eating disorder and WANTS her with me. I know her, she knows me. We have a relationship that I can't just break away from in an instant and cut off for good. I don't ever stick at recovery because I always feel as soon as I start eating more, I am going to lose my eating disorder or people won't think I even HAVE an eating disorder but OF COURSE I STILL DO. Just increasing my calories doesn't mean I don't have it anymore. It's always here and it's going to take a long journey to get rid of Ethel for good, and by that time, with the work I hopefully will have put in, that won't be scary anymore.

This was a big realisation for me today, because I hadn't ever really linked why I never stuck at recovery with those feelings before. So back to the famous bread roll. I was feeling rubbish yesterday, I took laxatives and I wanted to just cave in and go back to my eating disorder because it's all I've ever known for twelve years. But then I thought *no way*. So... I ATE THE BREAD ROLL! Did I weigh it? *Nope*. Do I know the calories in it? *Nope*. Did I still claw out the excess dough in the middle? *Yep*. Recovery isn't always about winning *every* little thing. I've made some progress and I got the roll; I didn't put it down and pick it up again twenty times, I just picked it up. I didn't weigh the roll, I didn't track the calories of the roll, and I didn't panic about the roll. Instead of just having tuna salad which is what I've been having for lunch all week, I had a tuna salad roll and that, for me, is *massive*.

Recovery is *tough*. It's *meant* to be <u>hard work</u>. If it was easy, we'd all be recovered, healthy beans enjoying food. It's GOING to take time and it's going to mean lots of back and forth, up and down, all over, struggles. Some days will be great, others not so. Some days I'll weigh the bread roll, some days I won't even be able to buy the bread roll. But some days, like today, I'll eat the bread roll and truly enjoy it, mostly guilt free. Recovery has so many hurdles. Recovery has so many strands. Recovery is a tree growing up ever so high with so many branches going off in all different directions. All obstacles and challenges, fails and trials. But eventually, one day, we're all going to be sitting at the very top of the tree, looking out into the distance, happy and free, at LIFE. Leonie xox

May 2019 – Blog

I'm having a really tough few days and I feel like I've been here so many times, of *wanting* to get better and *really* wanting it but then I just fall back into my eating disorder and now I'm already planning to low restrict tomorrow because I just feel I can't cope. I'm eating more and it's just making my anxiety ridiculous, I feel ridiculous, I feel emotional. I don't feel like I'm *ever* going to beat this, and I feel like my eating disorder is *always* going to win. I just want to be free. Leonie xox

May 2019 – Blog

Food anxiety is massive for us all and everyone's anxieties will be different. I saw a post this morning about someone challenging their anxiety around mayonnaise but who can eat a full hot meal. If you gave me a hot meal, my anxiety would be through the roof. So, everybody is different in what they get anxious over when it comes to their eating disorder. Today whilst I was jogging, I was thinking a bit more deeply about *why* I feel so anxious when it comes to eating hot meals and meals out and I think it's because of *this*. I have always had a fear of things that *aren't* in packets. I love packaged stuff because the packet gives me the nutritional information I need to feel comfortable eating the item. Now, I know nutritional information on packets is often inaccurate but still it provides me comfort and the ability to eat food. Home cooked meals are a massive fear of mine, as well as meals out and it's because I don't know the calorie information. They're foods often thrown together with random spices and sauces and that fills me with complete food anxiety and dread. Realising this today has helped a little – I know that in the past when I've gone out for meals, I've had to go to places where the calorie information is on the menu because it's helped me decide what to have and eased my anxiety. But my choice in what I want to eat should *not* be coming from what the nutritional information tells me. I should be choosing the meal based on what I *want* to eat. This is such a massive goal for me, because I want to be able to enjoy a full hot meal, but the food anxiety is massive.

Another realisation I had whilst jogging was if I check my step count because I'm ready to stop my jog, and it's in the next thousand (so from 1000 to 2002 etc) I will *have* to jog to the next thousand. I like to round it off in thousands and that's just the way I've always done my jogs. But some days, I'm *exhausted* and I want to stop early but my eating disordered brain won't let me. So, this is another massive goal I've given myself for this week to stop when I *feel* done instead of when I tell myself I *should* be done. I feel more positive for this week. Let a new fresh week of recovery BEGIN. Leonie xox

June 2019 – Blog

This week I've been challenging myself to eat foods I've wanted *in the moment*. That's meant a couple of ice creams here, a few bread rolls there. Monday and today I have eaten a lot. I'm talking three times what I usually feed my body. It's seven o'clock and I want to take laxatives. This is obviously the eating disordered voice but the recovery side of me is like, you're *never* going to get better if you don't push past these fears and do it anyway. If I keep taking laxatives as a comfort when I feel I've eaten 'too much', I'm never going to learn to just let the anxiety around food pass and sit with the food in my system. So tonight, despite the eating disorder literally SCREAMING AT ME, I am going to reject the laxatives and just deal with the bloating and whatever else I feel tomorrow. If I don't ever say no to the eating disorder, I am *never* going to get better. I am starting to learn that I need to just sit with the food and let it process and let the food anxiety go away by itself. It's the putting it into practice that I find difficult. My body isn't used to so much food in one sitting so to keep repeating this process and keep feeling this way is hard. But I need to keep doing it over and over otherwise I'm never going to get used to it.

There's also a massive part of me that wants to hide behind the eating disorder anxiety and fears and say "well best wait until another day to try that, best wait till an actual occasion to go for a meal out, best wait to get angel cake and have it in the house, best WAIT." There is *never* going to be a good time to face all these fears. I *must* go for it now otherwise I'm never going to beat this disease. I'm obviously petrified of gaining weight. I'm scared to be a heavier size, where my body naturally wants to sit because that means I may be 'fat.' I want to start going for meals out to challenge myself but as well as the eating disorder, I also have anxiety, and going out is a big thing for me *ANYWAY*, without throwing the food element in, so this is a really tough challenge for me.

I feel all over the place in my recovery and I have been watching people's YouTube recovery videos and they're all doing so well, which makes me feel as though I am failing. I think I have to remember though that I am only just beginning my recovery journey so of course my progress is going to be at a different level and there is no right or wrong way to do this. I need to delete my calorie counter. I need to get rid of my food scales. I can't even remember why I stupidly decided to buy them, I didn't always have them right from the start of this disease. The scales are a new thing and why did I have to add a new element in to my disorder? Why wasn't I satisfied just counting calories, when did my anxiety become so extreme that I had to weigh everything? How do people honestly go through their lives without weighing food, knowing the calories in their foods and not weighing themselves? How is that possible? I know it is, because people do it every day. I'm so determined to do this, but where do I even start. Do I just do it cold turkey? Do I do it in stages?

On Tuesday morning I was like "yeah come on let's do this." I put the weighing scales on top of my kitchen cupboards. I cannot tell you the sheer anxiety I had in the moments after I did this. I made a honey and lemon and started panicking because I didn't know the calories in the honey. Two hours later, the scales were back on the kitchen side and I was weighing my fruit for my smoothie. I feel OK though, I gave it a go, and I know I'll do it again, it's just *when*. Recovery is so time consuming and every little thing that healthy people find so easy is so hard with an eating disorder. I regret the day I ordered those scales. But I can't go back, only forward so I need to work on building up the courage to get rid of them for good.

I read a post today that said when you first start recovery, your body and mind are going to want to eat *everything*. The post made it very clear that **that is OK**. You want to eat everything because you've starved your body for so long. Your body and mind want everything in sight because you've spent years denying them essential nutrients and calories they need to simply survive and function properly.

I want to jump straight to recovered from eating disorder, so I can have food in the house and not feel the need to eat it all in one go. The point is though, that I need to *go through* the recovery and this process. The process of letting my body eat what it wants, when it wants, so that it learns to trust itself and its natural hunger again and let go of all these rules I've made for myself over the years.

Another thing I read is that your body doesn't care what weight you want to be at. We have this dream in our minds that we can be recovered at the low weight we want to be. NO. Our bodies *do not care* about what we want in our messed up eating disordered minds. Our body will just work to reach the weight it wants to be at. Our body knows what weight we need to be at and what weight we can maintain healthily without starving. I want the recovery but not the weight gain. Well that's ridiculous. I can't expect my body to stay the same whilst I'm starving it. If I want to have a healthy relationship with food and eat 'normally' again, then I need to be prepared that my body will physically change, grow and redefine itself when it realises I'm done hurting it. These things are *so hard to accept*. So hard to put into action and so hard to keep in mind on the days where my eating disorder makes me want to give up. But I need to push through and allow all these changes. **_Recovery is just so messy,_** but I feel I'm **starting** to get somewhere. Small steps. Leonie xox

June 2019 – Blog

Today I got dressed and went out and got myself an iced coffee despite the anxiety (general, social and eating disordered), telling me not to go into town 'just for coffee I don't need'. I shouldn't have it and people will be wondering why I'm just randomly ordering a coffee alone. I feel so proud that I just ignored the voices in my head that told me I shouldn't do it and I went and did it anyway.

I came home and then the anxiety reappeared because I've gained two pounds. I know two pounds isn't a massive amount, and I know that my body will keep gaining weight until it realises I'm not going to starve it anymore, and then it'll probably balance itself out somewhere between where I'm at now and a weight higher than I'd like which is where I'll probably get to during the recovery process. But this gain has set off so much anxiety in me because I'm so scared to gain weight. I know I need to just trust this process and allow my body to do its thing and get me to a healthy place but I'm struggling. Ethel shouts loud and tells me I shouldn't have got the iced latte because I've already gained weight and I should throw it away.

It's so hard because it's just a constant screaming match inside your mind and you never know who is going to win. I'm trying, but with every small step I take, like getting the latte, something always comes to rain on my parade. Leonie xox

July 2019 – Blog

These last two weeks have been difficult. After the two-pound gain, my brain *screamed* at me to restrict and I decided I'd go back to restriction. But then I kept waking up and thinking, no I can't live like this forever, I need to embrace this and just keep going with recovery. So, it's been a bit all over the place and I've had some positive days where I've felt good and healthy, and then other days where I've wanted to eat little. I've also had a few days where I've felt really pumped to face some challenges and fears but that haven't gone to plan. For example, I decided to go buy my favourite ice cream and was like "yep, let's do this, recovery is all about letting myself have these foods" but then I got to the shop and the shelf was empty. I freaked out, but I didn't want to use it as an excuse to *not* eat ice cream, so on the spot I chose different ice creams to buy and then I literally freaked out the whole way home. I cried at home because it wasn't the ice cream I'd 'allowed' myself in my head, the calories were all different, (not that it should matter), and I didn't know if I felt confident enough to eat the ice cream. It made me realise just how hard recovery is, in every way. It's going to be a long journey, but I am determined to succeed. Leonie xox

My last blog, July 2019

As I reflect on the year I've had and the blogs I've written, I can really see a personal growth in myself. I see where I was in 2018, and where I am now. I'm starting to climb towards health and I'm probably the best I've been in a long time, which has suddenly just fallen into place. A few months ago, I was deep into a relapse, eating five hundred calories a day and feeling guilty over everything I did. I wouldn't say yes to coffees out and I'd never buy foods I loved. Now I'm still working at recovery but I'm doing it with more power behind me, more zest to my lemon! I feel strong. I'm challenging things I've never challenged in my life. Like hot meals in the evening. Despite my intense fear of hot meals, I've been having salmon and salad with avocado or sweet potato over the last two weeks. I'm challenging myself daily to make bigger steps in my recovery, and not stay stuck in my safe zones.

I've come such a long way and it just goes to show, although this lemon will remain forever, it's starting to lose its mould. It's becoming yellow again; brighter, firmer, steadier and more confident and much more consistent. My recovery in my mental health has come such a long way, and with each day I win a little victory, I'm slowly getting stronger and my lemon has more of a zing to it. One day I am going to throw this lemon in the bin and it'll be gone forever. I am ready for life to finally begin.

Making Lemonade

2020

What is life beyond the eating disorder? Beyond the mental illness, beyond all the lemons in my life so far? Well, in the last year alone, my life has been full of so many different experiences and changes, all of which I'm truly thankful for. I moved, I started being able to leave the house properly again, after feeling trapped for so long in my anxiety. I made the decision to start my degree, *finally*, at twenty-seven. I decided to put my daughter in childcare two days a week so I could take some time for *me*. My Mum wasn't that happy at this choice, because of her own negative experience with my little sister. The thing is though, at some point, I needed to stop letting the opinions of others make me feel guilty for my own choices. I know that self-care is extremely important, and perhaps she doesn't. Perhaps that's a journey *she* needs to take to find her own lemonade. I know that I need some time each week to focus on myself, sit down, read a book, have a bath, go for a run, look up at the sun shining through the clouds and take a deep breath and be thankful for all I have. Start painting again, drawing again, *creating* again. I've made my own decisions in this last year, without trying to please everyone, without walking on eggshells, without feeling inadequate or that I have no power. I've made a life for myself that I am comfortable and happy with, and that I work hard towards daily.

Life beyond all these lemons has given me *hope* again. For a long time, as you'll have read, Mrs C was my hope, because she kept me from falling into the darkest place. She's remained a constant support in my life and I owe her everything I am today. After her, the next big person in my life was my ex-husband. I relied on Frankie for hope, for care, for love. Then he let me down and broke my trust and it took a long time to rebuild myself again. What I learnt from that rebuild is that I need to be my own source of hope. To give myself all the care, love, support and belief that I tried to get from others. Once I realised that, I began to heal from the inside out. These days, the eating disorder and the anxiety are softly spoken, and no longer scream inside my head. I no longer feel such powerful self-hate, and it's because I've taken the time to let myself feel all the mould, and to heal from it. It certainly wasn't an easy journey, and to all on the outside, I don't think I look any different. I feel it though, on the inside and that's really where it counts. I may never have a perfectly shaped nose, or a perfect jaw line. My boobs unfortunately aren't in their perky teens anymore, and although I jog, my legs are far from toned. I may not look exactly how I'd like on the outside, and that's something I'm still working on, but on the inside, I've healed so much, and that's more important.

Whilst creating these blogs, I genuinely thought I had found 'food freedom' and full recovery. I realise now though, that I was still in the dreaded cycle of relapse and quasi recovery. It is only now, months into 2020, that I have found full recovery and true freedom. Of course, I still have hard days, but I have healed my mind, and that allows me to move past the hard days with gentle self-love and respect. I still face difficulties, like the fact that Alissa *still* will not sleep all night long, even though she is almost three years old now. During those moments, deep into the early hours of the morning, when I am so exhausted and tearful, I take a deep breath, I say a prayer and I remember the wise words of my midwife Sam, who once told me as long as I got four hours a night, I would be able to survive. I am surviving. Every. Single. Day.

The ability to *feel* is so powerful and so wonderful, and I don't know why I spent so many years trying to supress the painful parts. I love to feel all emotions now, because it reminds me of who I am. This newfound happiness has allowed me to become *me* again, with no filter or trying to live up to other people's standards. This has meant that I've embarked on a journey back to my religious roots and have been able to develop a relationship with God again. I'm not here to talk about religion or judge religion or take judgement about religion. Religion is so personal, and so precious and that's all I'll say about it. The focus is that it's made me happy and it's helped me to heal and for now, that's all I care about.

I've also been able to think long and hard about what *I* want to do in my life. For a long time, I tried to please so many people. Work full time so there was always money to spend and live fancy, work part time so I could help out with family things and keep myself mentally stable; study away, study near to home, study nursing because studying midwifery limits your choices; learn to drive, fail my test, feel pressure to learn again. The list of trying to please everybody goes on and on. In the end, I discovered who I am, without everybody else chiming in. I learnt I don't enjoy driving at all, and so I never did retake that test. I learnt that I never wanted to go off to university far away, and that is OK. I learnt that I didn't ever want to be a nurse, even if it was the sensible option to choose. I learnt that I could be a fantastic counsellor one day if I choose to go back and do my last course. For now, though,

I'm studying Religious Studies and I *will* make my goal of becoming a teacher, just like I wrote in my diary in Year Seven, long before mental illness found me.

The biggest thing I've learnt though, is that there is *no* greater love on this earth than that of a mother's love for her child. Having Alissa was the hardest and most rewarding thing I've ever done. Gaining weight and having people constantly looking at me, touching me, complimenting me on how 'big' I was, all made pregnancy so mentally challenging. Swollen feet, back ache, tiredness, losing Dad, being unable to starve as a coping mechanism, all made pregnancy unbearable at times. Giving birth to Alissa and having such complications and not having my Mum there at the end and going through so much was emotionally exhausting. From day one though of her little life, she has only ever filled me with pure love, happiness and joy. She completely coated my heart and my soul and every moment we've had together in her two years has been so remarkable and rewarding. If nothing else good ever happens to me, I know she'll always be enough and with her, I know I can achieve every goal, every recovery step, and every bit of living my life.

I've realised I don't want to keep gathering lemons. I feel done with lemons. I just want to make lemonade now; boring, bland, lemonade, perhaps with a zesty sharp twist. I am done with obstacles, challenges and destruction and I welcome peace, happiness and health like I never have before. I want a simple, boring life, just me and my baby and it is now that time. I am ready and I am done collecting lemon after lemon. I am ready to just be lemonade. Don't get me wrong, learning how to make lemonade is hard. It requires learning how to throw all the mouldy lemons in the bin, knowing that you've acknowledged them, felt them, deeply understood them, and then let them go. They're not right for you now. You need ripe, firm lemons for this glass. I think that's the key to this whole happy life lark. If you can't let the past go, you'll never truly be able to move on. If you're always looking behind you, you'll always be missing out on seconds of what's in front of you. I could easily stay in the past, cry over Dad every day, relapse in my eating disorder repeatedly, relive the pain and sadness that love brought me, and the trauma that birth gave me. Or, I could choose to look in front and see the wonderful life that I have now. Studying for something I truly want to do, living my best life with my growing baby, who surprises and makes me smile every day. Getting to create precious memories with dear friends and grow closer to family. Getting to experience the warmth that finding myself has brought me, and the warmth that others have given me along the way. Making lemonade is all about seeing the bad lemons but not letting them get into your glass. Choose the good ones, focus on them, and make every single day a fresh tall glass of lemonade. Life is waiting for you and you're wasting precious time. Don't look back, don't keep picking the mouldy lemons back up. Throw them away after you've truly felt them and experienced them and focus on what's in front. Well, what are you waiting for? Put this load of old rubbish that you're reading down and go. *Live*.

Acknowledgements

Throughout all the craziness, I've been truly blessed in my life to experience such warmth, kindness and love from so many special people.

I'd like to thank Janet for giving me the inspiration to put all my ramblings together. Also, Emma, a big thank you for the sound advice and for always providing pick me up emojis in times of distress.

Mrs C and Mrs W, you two deserve a hideous amount of wine from me for the support you both gave me when I needed it most. I won't ever be able to thank you both enough, but I hope this helps a little.

My incredible friends deserve such tremendous thanks for being there through every battle and every adventure. Lauren, my fatty, you have been there by my side since Year Five and you have shared every moment with me. You have been the best friend I could have ever hoped to meet, and I will never be able to express how thankful I am for you. Megan, meeting you at college was such a blessing. For over ten years, you have been there for me every single day, giving me advice, encouragement and McDonald's in times of need. Having a best friend with no mental health issues who can give such balanced and calming advice is such a beautiful find, and I'm so glad I found you. My newest best friend, Damaris – there are honestly no words for how I feel about you. I am so thankful to Jehovah for sending you to me, for giving me someone who brings the scripture to life; "a true friend shows love at all times and is a brother who is born for times of distress." Proverbs 17:17 You came into my life because Jehovah knew I needed you and I will never be able to thank Him enough. I have many other lovely friends; Mandy and Brenda, who come every week to give me spiritual nourishment, and Jen, who gives me the best cooking advice and let's our children wreck her house so beautifully.

Having friends and family is so important, and my family have always stuck by me. I'll never forget my Mum telling me that friends come and go, but family will always be there. They certainly have been. Jan, Ashleigh, Daisy, Alissa and Mum. You guys are my home. Emmie, Charlotte, Amelia, Abby – you are some of my craziest cousins, all with such beautiful personalities. But Mum is the one who deserves the most thanks.

Mum, words won't ever be able to express how much love I have for you. You are our glue, our love, our home. We need you and love you more than you'll ever know. Thank you for building a solid relationship with me, one that stands so strong now. Thank you for never giving up on me, even though I was a terrible teenager and used to steal your wine. Thank you for always being there, despite me not always reaching out to you. Really it just boils down to thank you. For being *Mum*.

Lastly, Dad. You're not here, but now your memory will always be kept alive. I love and miss you every single day.

~

Printed in Great Britain
by Amazon

42504624R00121